WHAT NEXT?

THE MILLENNIAL'S GUIDE TO SURVIVING AND THRIVING IN THE REAL WORLD

Michael Price

What Next? Copyright © 2013 by Michael Price

All rights reserved. No part of this publication may be reproduced, distributed, or transmitted in any form or by any means, including photocopying, recording, or other electronic or mechanical methods, without the prior written permission of the publisher, except in the case of brief quotations embodied in critical reviews and certain other noncommercial uses permitted by copyright law.

Bulk discount ordering information:

Special discounts are available for high quantity purchases by corporations, associations, book stores and others. For details visit: www.pricelessmg.com.

To book Michael Price for an event or speaking engagement visit: www.pricelessmg.com.

First Edition

Priceless Media Group

ISBN: 978-0-9892947-0-6 (hbk.)

ISBN: 978-0-9892947-1-3 (pbk.)

ISBN: 978-0-9892947-2-0 (dig.)

Table of Contents

Chapter 1: Welcome to the Real World   1
- History Lesson   7
- Demographics   8
- Characteristics   12
- Prosperity   15
- Technology   22

Chapter 2: The Internet Age   27
- Education   29
- Social Networking   35
- Real World Networking   43
- Building a Business   46
- Turning Passion into Profit   48

Chapter 3: High School   51
- Exploration   53
- Extracurricular   57
- Volunteering   60
- Internships   61

Chapter 4: Higher Education   65
- Is College Right For You?   67
- Antiquated Education   72
- The True Value of a College Education   76

Chapter 5: Build a Brand   81
- Start a Blog   84
- Social Networking   88
- Develop a Portfolio   90
- Work for Free   91

Chapter 6: Surviving Corporate America   97
- Know Your Role   99
- Know Your Worth   100
- Get in Good   102
- Be Valuable   103
- Nights and Weekends   104
- Leadership   105
- Bring People Together   106
- Transparency   107
- Whiners vs. Winners   108
- Cut Throat   109
- More Money More Problems   110
- Interviewing   110
- Contracting   113
- Job vs. Career   114
- Employment vs. Entrepreneurship   114

Chapter 7: Escaping Corporate America   119
- Business 101   122
- Savings   125
- Risk   127
- Plan   129

Chapter 8: Financial Literacy   133
- Preparation   136
- First Job Jitters   138
- Tracking Expenses   141
- How to Split Bills   144
- Managing and Monitoring Your Credit   146

Chapter 9: Message to Parents   153
- Respect for Authority   155
- Building Leaders   157
- Valuing the Dollar   158

Conclusion: The World is ours for the Taking   163

Thank You   166

Appendix A: Checklist   169
Appendix B: Resources   175
Appendix C: Research   183

Endorsements

"If you're a Millennial wondering 'what next' in your life, this book is for you. Michael Price has been there and done that, and offers his advice in a no-nonsense style readers will love."

- **Barbara Corcoran**
   Star of ABC's Shark Tank

"Are you a Millennial? Confused about life? This book is your answer."

- **Andrew Warner**
   Founder of Mixergy

"Use any and all resources – including this wonderful book, What Next? The Millennial's Guide to Surviving and Thriving in the Real World – to study and practice as you create the future you desire and deserve. To author Michael Price… Well done!"

- **Winn Claybaugh**
   Dean & Cofounder of Paul Mitchell Schools
   Author of BE NICE (OR ELSE!)

"In an era of new technology, a new economy, and new opportunities, Michael Price shows us what it takes to create a life of meaning as part of a Millennial generation that is ready to make a huge positive impact on the world."

- **Ryan Allis**
   Co-founder of iContact
   CEO of Connect.com

Forward

As a happy, successful Baby Boomer born in 1959, I love my generation. I also love my parents' generation, because they raised me to be hardworking, honest, aware of others, and nice. However, as a businessman, I am also smart enough to know that my future success relies heavily on today's generation—the Millennials! I have therefore studied about them, studied with them, worked and played with them, and done all I can to "enter their world" so I can share with them the good things from my generation, just as my parents did for me in sharing the ethics and life lessons of their generation. Unlike some colleagues of my own age who express harsh opinions about Millennials, I find them to be humble learners, passionate philanthropists, and creative entrepreneurs. I also find them to be patriotic, globally aware, loyal to family and friends, and hardworking employees.

My message to Millennials: The world is at your feet but you must work really, really hard to achieve happiness and success, however you define it. The good news for you is that the hard work I endorse does not have to be misery. In fact, you are the generation of balance! Along with your hard work, take all of your other valued attributes, attitudes, and life skills with you on your journey. Use any and all resources – including this wonderful book, What Next? The Millennial's Guide to Surviving and Thriving in the Real World – to study and practice as you create the future you desire and deserve. To author Michael Price… Well done!

— Winn Claybaugh

Dean & Cofounder of Paul Mitchell Schools

Author of BE NICE (OR ELSE!)

Dedication

This book would not be possible without my dynamic DNA and my wonderful wife. Without the wisdom, guidance, and insane work ethic drilled into me by my parents, grandparents, and all those who came before them, I would be nothing! And to my lovely wife Michelle, you've been there for me, supported me, believed in me, and had faith in me even when I lost faith in myself. You are my other half. You complete me.

Chapter 1: Welcome to the Real World

Are You Ready?

My fellow Millennials, are you prepared for the real world? Do you have what it takes to not only survive, but thrive? Do you know exactly what you want to do with your life? Do you know what college you want to attend? Do you even want to go to college? Why do you want to go to college? Is college worth the tremendous debt incurred? Did you go to college, drop out or graduate and are still confused about your career? Are you prepared for 10 - 12 hour work days? Do you know how to manage finances? Do you understand how credit works? Are you mentally and emotionally prepared to accept and excel in the challenges the real world will bring? If you answered no or are unsure of your answer to the preceding questions, then you need some assistance. If you answered yes, then you are either full of it and haven't yet experienced the Real World or you are among a rare few Millennials who actually "get it." I'm going to make a huge assumption that a majority of the Millennials reading this book who answered the preceding questions honestly, either answered no or unsure to the questions above.

Hello. My name is Michael Price. Nine years ago I graduated from high school and had no idea what to do next. I was super ambitious but wasn't sure how to best capitalize on my ambition. I didn't know if college was the route to go, entrepreneurship, or joining the workforce straight out of high school and climbing my way to the top. I chose to do all of the above. After high school at the age of 18 I went to college and realized that the college system in its current form wasn't equipped to properly educate me for the career I wanted to pursue. After my freshmen year of college I dropped out, taught myself web design, search engine marketing, and social media marketing. At 21, I landed my first real job at a digital marketing agency in Dallas, TX earning $48,000/year as a social media manager. While working at this agency, I had the opportunity to lead strategy, initiation, and execution of social media campaigns for small tech start ups, brick and mortar businesses and a few big businesses. From 23 to 27 I worked as a freelance and in-house social media marketing consultant, consulting some of the biggest businesses in their industries. In these four years as a consultant, I reached an income of over $60,000/year, which is more than double the average income earned by most Americans in my age bracket. Based on my level and years of experience, I'm projected to earn over six-figures/year before I reach the age of 30. I've achieved all of this without a college degree and did I mention I'm debt free? At the time of writing this book, I was 27 years old. Am I telling you all of this to brag? Absolutely not! Even though the success I've achieved at my age (despite not having a college degree) is more than twice that of others in my age group, I don't hold this level of success as something that defines me. In fact, I often criticize myself for not being more financially successful at my age than I am.

4 | What Next?

The reason I felt compelled to give my performance report is to illustrate that I know what it takes to do the following:

- Pursue your passion
- Accomplish your goals
- Maximize your potential
- Manage your finances

And to sum it all up... Survive and thrive in the Real World!

I wrote this book to share my experiences and expertise' in handling the unique and tremendous set of challenges that my generation faces in the Real World. It's very important that Millennials understand the historic and generational differences that will determine the success or failure of their lives based on the world we live in today. The rules for achieving success in our parents' generation no longer apply, just as the rules for achieving success in our grandparents' generation didn't apply to our parents.

The world today moves and changes much faster than ever before. Consumer buying trends change over the course of a year as opposed to a decade, and new technology makes previous technology obsolete in a matter of months as opposed to years. The Internet was the game changer that changed life as we know it and no other segment of the population is more affected by this than Millennials. The Internet is a super highway of Information. As I mentioned above, I'm a college dropout who self taught myself skills that I learned on the Internet that have allowed me to earn a living that's double that of my peers. That's the world we live in today. In yesterdays' generation, you didn't find nearly as many millionaires, billionaires, and entrepreneurs as you do today and why? Because the world is truly global now. The walls have come crumbling down thanks to the World Wide Web and this game change is the defining difference in the Millennial Generation as compared to generations prior. So who are Millennials?

Millennials are young adults born between the late 1970s and early 2000s, allowing for an age range between 12 - 35 years old present day (2013).

Since 1993, there have been a lot of people who have talked about us, written articles about us, and made predictions about us, but none of these writers and journalists have been us.

By writing this book I am changing that, by providing insight about Millennials from a Millennials' perspective. As a Millennial who has survived and thrived, I have a unique perspective to provide that Gen X analysts, writers, and journalists do not have as outsiders. In this book, I have taken my life lessons from the ages of 15 - 27 and have provided them to my generation as a guide of things to do and not to do. My hope and intent is that I can somehow assist others who are lost in the world without guidance to maximize their potential and achieve success. Although monetarily I have achieved success at a young age by most people's standards, I believe that success is not dictated by how much money you earn, but by the level of your happiness. I believe it is better to be a starving artist than to be an over-fed corporate clown.

This book is entitled "What Next?" because it follows a sequence of events that allows Millennials to figure out what's next, beginning in high school, post high school, college, and on into the "Real World." No matter what part of this path in life you are currently on, you can read this book and make some modifications or adjustments to your life that will allow you to survive and thrive.

This is the book I always hoped would be written but never was. I've read dozens of books throughout the years following high school hoping to find bits and pieces of the information contained within this book. I learned the lessons in this book the hard way, through trial and error while attending the School of Hard Knocks. A.K.A. The Real World. I've taken these lessons and I give them back to you. The people. My generation.

History Lesson

"Who knows only his generation remains always a child"

- George Norlin

What a great quote to start this chapter with. I believe this quote to be tremendously powerful and relevant, especially for the Millennial Generation (Generation Y) which has commonly been referred to as the "Me Generation." This adjective has been used to describe the often times selfish and disregarded attitudes of Millennials. As a Millennial, I can say without a shadow of a doubt, we are definitely selfish and we can quite frequently be known to disregard others.

I felt it critical to include and start this book off with a history lesson, because you can't know where you're going, unless you know where you came from. I believe that if Millennials have a better grasp of the historical differences that separate us from previous generations, we will be able to better understand the Real World and better understand ourselves.

Demographics

Millennials are taking over, or should I say, we've already taken over. We're the largest generation of young people since the 1960s and we're 80 million strong making us 1/3 of the total U.S. population. We love spending our money on fancy gadgets and gizmos and we love spending our parents' money on gadgets and gizmos even more! A majority of our parents are baby boomers, born between the years of 1946 - 1964. Much like us, our parents were very money motivated. Our grandparents built the foundation of the middle class and our parents solidified it.

Ambition and desire to have more "things," has been the cultural progression that has increased from one generation to the next. In our grandparents' generation, products were built with quality and were meant to last for years or even decades. Don't believe me? Go into your grandmothers' kitchen and I guarantee that you will find an original Kitchen Aid Mixer that still works like it did 35 years ago. Go in the back of her closet and pull out her old sewing machine; I bet it still works as well. Now fast forward to our parents' generation. Once the middle class became solidified by our parents' generation, product manufacturers quickly realized that with the sharp increase in rising household incomes, there was no need to make durable, long-lasting, well-built products anymore. This change in product quality spawned (in my opinion) the mass consumerism of American culture today, and no generation is more susceptible to accepting poorly built products than Millennials. No longer are products made of tin, steel, and other durable materials. Products of today are generally made of cheap plastics and composite materials. I'm taking you down this path of understanding the evolution of consumer spending changes and product manufacturing changes because it points out one of the biggest differences that separate Millennials from generations before us. It's our insatiable appetite and acceptance of rapid change. We generally don't get bothered or change our spending habits just because something new comes out that makes the previous version we bought six months to one year prior obsolete. We embrace change. When you begin to see and understand how our embrace of rapid change in products affects us, it becomes easy to see why political change and social change happens so rapidly. In my 27 short years of life I've witnessed rapid social and political change that my generation has been largely involved in pushing forward. In just the last ten years, I've witnessed the election of America's first black President. Acceptance of the LGBT community/movement has gone from radical opposition to wide spread acceptance. Religious extremism has been exposed, and politicians have begun to lose power as they've become more exposed as well.

When Barack Obama launched his 2008 campaign for Presidency with his theme of change, it wasn't just about Washington Politics. It was a theme that many Millennials identified with in every aspect of life, and the younger you were in 2008, the more likely you were to believe in and feel this message of change. Whether you like or dislike Barack Obama is irrelevant. However, it is worth noting that Barack Obama's Presidential Campaign was successful largely due to his massive support from eligible Millennial voters.

I believe that when the next generation rises up and Millennials begin to be referenced in history books, I believe one word will be used to describe us. I believe that word will be change. Not because of Barack Obama, but because of our extreme willingness to be open-minded to the rapid acceptance of change.

One pivotal social epidemic that makes Millennials so accepting of change and open-mindedness is our integrated ethnic and culturally diverse childhoods. Despite what the mainstream media often likes to suggest, our generation has had very limited racial and ethnic inequality. As children in grade school, Millennials attend school with a wide range of different people from diverse cultural and ethnic backgrounds. This has had a tremendous affect on our ability to be more open-minded and accepting of different types of people. When I was in grade school all the way up into high school, I had friends from all different backgrounds, ethnicities, and religious affiliations. Some of my best friends were white, black, Asian, Indian, Jewish,

European, and Hindu. I even dated girls from different racial and ethnic backgrounds and married a white Catholic woman of German, English, and Italian descent. I myself come from a diverse ethnic background. My father is black and my mother is half black and half Japanese.

With "Change" being the defining term I believe Millennials will be credited with in the history books, I feel so incredibly proud and grateful to be apart of this generation. One could argue that if you look at the biggest social, cultural, and political challenges America and the rest of the world face today, it could largely be tied to the current generation that is running the world who remains reluctant to embrace change. This (in my opinion) is what defines the Baby Boomers and the generation before them. They are often times set in their ways and beliefs, effectively stifling social, cultural, and political progress. The world today and America more specifically is still "owned and operated" by Baby Boomers and the generation before them.

When Millennials take the reigns, I believe our basic attitudes of acceptance, open-mindedness, and willingness to accept change will be the defining moment in history that will re-shape America and the rest of the world.

Characteristics

What are some characteristics that define Millennials? This is the part of the book where I begin to get honest and interpersonal about who we are as a generation and what generally defines us. Some of the adjectives are nice and some are harsh, but they are all honest.

- Selfish
- Ambitious
- Open-Minded
- Narcissistic
- Self-Centered
- Worldly
- Socially-Conscious
- Informed
- Sense of Entitlement
- Powerful

Those are some pretty big words right? I believe those ten words best describe our generation.

Here's a true story that I heard on a talk radio show a few years ago about a father (James) and his son (Jared), who just so happens to be a Millennial. This story describes our generation perfectly!

James' son Jared plays on a little league soccer team. Jared's soccer team won every game in their season and went on to play in the championship tournament. James is the head coach of Jared's soccer team. Before the game, Jared expressed to his dad how nervous he was about playing the rival team. He felt like they were better than his team. James told Jared, "Don't worry son. Just get out there and do your best. At the end of the game everyone on both teams will receive the same trophy for participating and getting this far in the tournament." After having this father/son conversation, Jared joined his team who were also nervous about the game. Jared told his teammates, "Hey guys. Don't be nervous. Even if we lose, we still get the same trophy." Jared's team lost the game.

After hearing this story, I couldn't help but think to myself, would Jared's team have won or at least tried harder if they weren't put at ease by receiving the same reward for losing as they would for winning?

This story has Millennial written all over it. This is how we were raised. I remember being in grade school and having an annual assembly every year in which teachers would hand out awards and certificates to students. At these assemblies, parents of the students would sit in the back of the auditorium smiling in joy and snapping pictures as their kids won awards. We had achievement-oriented awards for being on the A-Honor Roll, A/B-Honor Roll, and then we also had ridiculous awards for perfect attendance and good behavior. Even as a 1st grader I thought this was ridiculous! I was on the A-Honor Roll every year. I achieved something and earned my award. Why were kids getting awards for perfect attendance and good behavior? These are things you're supposed to do by default. You shouldn't receive an award, gold star, or any recognition whatsoever for doing what you should be doing anyway. Now just stop and think about giving someone an award for good behavior. Are they training these children to become prison inmates? Good behavior is the term used to provide inmates recognition and a reward of time reduction off of their prison sentence.

The greatest detriment to the Millennial Generation that has led to our greatest character flaw is our sense of entitlement. We often believe that we should receive a reward just for participating or showing up. This has led to a generational epidemic of laziness, lack of ambition, lack of desire, and a lack of accountability.

It's very difficult for me to understand this paradox, as I wasn't raised to feel any sense of entitlement whatsoever. My parent's were hard working, college educated, and no non-sense. In my household, I was rewarded for getting straight A's. I wasn't rewarded for going to school everyday and showing up on time, and I certainly wasn't rewarded for respecting my teachers and not talking back to them. These things were expected of me. Here's the interesting oxymoron though, even though I wasn't raised to be praised for doing default duties, I somehow adopted a sense of entitlement myself. My sense of entitlement is extremely low. However, I often times want things done my way and I want them done the easiest and quickest way possible, and in some instances I might even feel I deserve a round of applause. Yep! That's Millennials. That's how we are. That's who we are, and even though I pride myself in not being as narcissistic, egotistical, entitled, and self-centered as my peers, I too must admit that I have those character flaws as well. I certainly didn't break the mold.

Prosperity

Prosperity or the lack thereof is an issue that many analysts and journalists have feared for our generation. At the height of the recession from 2008 - 2010, many of my peers were graduating from college. As they left college and looked to enter the workforce, they were met with the harsh realities of life. They were young, inexperienced, and we were in the middle of a down economy. Instead of transitioning from college dorm room to apartment, most college graduates between 2008 to present day have found themselves transitioning from dorm room to bedroom at mom and dad's house.

The hopes and dreams of having the almighty "piece of paper," (college degree) just hasn't been good enough for Millennials to secure jobs. I have friends and family who are Millennials, who have MBA's from accredited colleges, and they still can't find employment or salaries that are high enough to allow them to prosper, grow their savings and pay off their student loan debt. This is not an isolated incident. This situation is systemic, and I believe that unless our education system modernizes itself, the American Dream will largely be out of reach for Millennials. I'm no economist, but I do have eyes, and I pay very close attention to trends. Down economy or up economy, economic prosperity is getting worse and it's so systemic that there isn't just one entity to blame. Blame can be placed on our antiquated and factory-oriented education system that spits out millions of robots with the same attributes disallowing them to be competitive in the job market; an extreme and continuingly increasing rise in inflation; excessive government intervention in business; lack of government oversight in Federal spending; and a disconnection between business needs misaligning with core curriculum in our education system.

Before I continue to depress you with my apocalyptic vision of America's future, I must stress and emphasize that America is still the greatest place on Earth. No where else in the world can you be what you want to be and achieve what you want to achieve. As long as you have a strong work ethic and a desire to succeed, America still has plenty of opportunity and economic prosperity. However, it takes a very special kind of person to rise above the disadvantages our generation has when compared to previous generations.

When I paint a negative canvas about future prosperity in America, I'm speaking purely in terms of the ability to prosper while being average. During the Baby Boomer Generation, they had a very simple formula:

Go to college + Graduate + Get married + Combine incomes + Invest in 401K & retirement fund = Retirement at 65 with a condo in South Florida.

That pipe dream is over, and even what seemed to be a dream 15 - 20 years ago for Baby Boomers has turned out to be a nightmare for many. Ask your parents how their retirement accounts look right now? They were probably wiped out as a result of the near economic collapse of the Great Recession. Ask your parents how much their house is worth today? I bet it has probably lost value, leaving them upside down which means they will have to pay to sell their house or face foreclosure.

Even though many Baby Boomers in their golden years are

not seeing a bright light towards retirement, they at least had what appeared to be a successful plan. All they had to do was be responsible and follow a few simple steps as outlined in the formula previously mentioned.

Our generation will not be privileged to receive pensions, 401K's, company sponsored retirement plans or even social security, Medicare, or Medicaid. This means that our generation more than any other generation prior must be ten times more financially responsible and more money cautious. I hate to say it, but the deck is stacked against us. Given the fact that our generation spends the highest proportion of our income on discretionary spending when compared to previous generations, we are in trouble, because in addition to the challenges we face from external forces, we are also our own worst enemy.

In case I haven't frightened you enough, here's some stats that should immediately knock you off your feet:

1966 – 2011:
- Incomes for bottom 90% of Americans grew by $59
- Incomes for top 10% of Americans grew by $116,071
- Incomes for top 1% of Americans grew by $366,623 (Source: David Cay Johnston for Tax Analysts)

Wages and Compensation Stagnation:

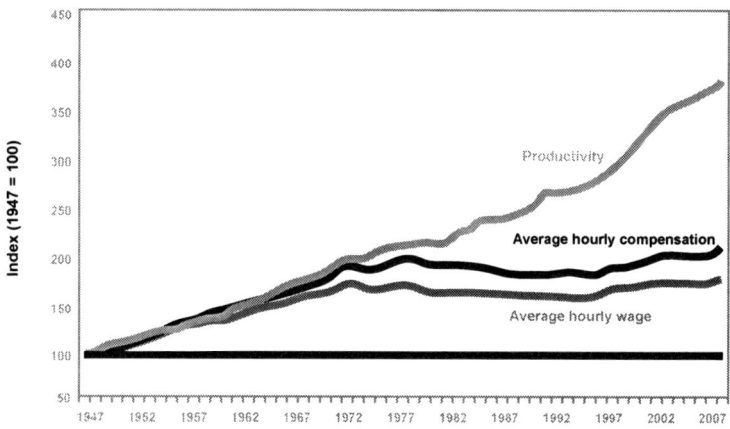

(Source: EPI analysis of Bureau of Economic Analysis and Bureau of Labor and Statistics)

In case you don't understand what's going on between the bullet points and the line graph, allow me to break it down for you. This data represents the complete collapse of the American Dream and demise for the American worker. For the past forty years the average working American has contributed unbelievable increases in work productivity and in exchange they've received stagnant wages. This isn't about rich vs. poor, middle class vs. high class, or distribution of wealth. This is about the future of America and determining where you fit in the big picture. My ambition is to be a part of the top 1% and your ambition should be just the same. While it's mathematically and realistically impossible that the majority of us will be in the top 1%, that doesn't mean you shouldn't strive for it or at least get serious about your financial future, unless of course you enjoy increased workloads with flat-lining compensation. Increases in inflation with stagnant wages is simply unsustainable, and if this trend continues America will see an entire generation reach their Golden years without the financial means to retire. What happens when millions of senior citizens can no longer physically work, they're financially broken, and social security has dried up? Do you understand how serious this is? Are you beginning to understand why being average no longer works? Are you beginning to see the veil of deceit that's been forced over our eyes?

In order to make it beyond being the "Average American," you must go beyond the status quo. You must reinvent yourself into something entirely different. You must rise!

Now is the time to be remarkable! Being average no longer works and achieving the financial prosperity our parents achieved, albeit an illusion, is going to be harder than ever before.

Since the height of the recession, home building has dropped to historic lows and apartment developments have risen to historic highs. Within the last ten years there's even been a new kind of apartment developed. It's called the "luxury apartment!" Ooh la la! That sounds so sexy right? So what do you get with a luxury apartment? You get fake hardwood floors, fake granite countertops, and an illusion of luxury wrapped up in cheap architecture and cheap building materials all for the ridiculous price of 30 - 40% higher rent payments when compared to apartments a decade ago. The mainstream media has been hyping our generation up and preparing our generation for this "New America" for the last eight years.

I like Ikea. I think they have some pretty neat things and I love New York, but I do not believe the future of American living should be confined to 400 sq. ft. "luxury apartments." I don't think there's anything cute and sexy about living in a modern cracker box where my bed folds down from the wall and my living room moonlights as my bedroom. No thanks!

But I've got news for you Generation Y. This is what life will be like for people within our generation who choose to be average. They will be renters and debtors for the rest of their life. If you want to see what life is like raising a family in a tiny apartment, then look at Eastern Europe. This is America New.0 as I like to call it. They plan to stack us on top of each other in tiny apartments so that we own nothing, but accept it as a result of the facade that is... "luxury apartment living."

By now you're probably thinking I'm a conspiracy theorist far-right psychopath. I'm not. I'm simply preparing you for one possible path your life may go down dependent on the choices you make at the most critical part of your life, which is your youth. The decisions you make from ages 15 - 25 will likely determine the outlook on the rest of your life, so make your decisions carefully.

As I dive into future chapters, I will discuss and share with you the exact things I've done that have allowed me to not only survive but thrive despite the madness and chaos going on in the world today. As of the writing of this book it is the beginning of 2013, and some analysts and economists say we're still in a recession. Despite the loss of prosperity in America in these last few years, I've excelled tremendously regardless of the odds stacked against me. I have no college degree, I'm young, and we're still in the midst of a down economy with a relatively high unemployment rate. In the last two years I've seen my income and opportunities skyrocket. As you continue to read this book, I'll tell you exactly how I've beaten the odds. You'll be happy to find that there is light at the end of the tunnel despite our generations' unique challenges.

Technology

In the last section about prosperity, I spoke quite a lot

about the negative outlook of America's financial future. One thing that can and likely will change all of that is the continual and rapid improvement of technology. I'm not just talking about the ability for Apple to make their hardware smaller so that they can shave off an extra couple of millimeters from your precious iPhone. I'm talking about artificial intelligence, medical advancements, ecommerce advancements, product advancements, automotive advancements, and alternative energy advancements. All of these industries are on the rise and as major advancements in these industries continue to be made, an abundance of new jobs will open up.

Many Americans often worry about the Rise of China. China (at this point) doesn't concern me. I believe every country that's involved in the global economy has a unique purpose, and I believe each of these countries know their purpose. Sure, a majority of the products in your home are made in China. However, these products are designed and developed by American businesses and sold to consumers globally. One thing America has always done and will always continue to do is lead the world in technological innovation. It's just apart of our DNA. It's a result of our freedom and Capitalistic society. As long as America continues to maintain freedom and Capitalism, we will continue to reign supreme and opportunity will continue to be available.

This rise in technological advancements positions our generation to not only be prepared for the jobs of the future, but to excel! Technology for Millennials is second-nature. Go to YouTube and search: "baby using smartphone." You will find tons of videos of babies and toddlers using smartphones and tablets with ease; before Millennials can even talk or walk, we're pre-wired to understand and embrace technology. The Baby Boomers on the other hand were well into their 40s and beyond when the tech boom began and personal computers became fully mainstream.

When I think about technology and advancement, I fall in love with this great nation all over again. It reminds me that there's hope, and that without any government influence or big business initiative, advancements of all kinds rather they be technology, social, political or economic will always happen in America.

The historical differences in the Millennial Generation compared to previous generations have a stark contrast and we have some difficult challenges ahead of us. Our journeys will not be easy. Traditional wisdom and guidance provided to our generation by our educational institutions and our parents are no longer good enough. Teachers, professors, and parents can give you a tremendous amount of guidance and good advice, but they are not equipped to help navigate you through the unique challenges our generation faces. It is to no fault of their own, and it shouldn't be expected that these authority figures give you the answers to life's trials and tribulations. Our parents and our educators aren't apart of our generation. They do not know the struggles we face and will continue to face, because there's a generation gap. Having walked all paths including college, entrepreneurship, and Corporate America as a Millennial still in his late youth, I believe I'm uniquely positioned to help guide our generation. I feel it is my responsibility. It is my destiny.

We will do this together. We will succeed. I will not accept our generation to be written off in history books as the "Me Generation." We are better than that.

We will shake up the world!

Chapter 2: The Internet Age

Freedom at Your Finger Tips

The Internet. It's arguably the most impactful technological development in human history. Sure, the automobile allowed us longer distance travel and the telephone allowed us to communicate with one another across local, state, national, and eventually international boundaries. However, no other advancement in human history has connected the planet the way the Internet has.

Being children of the "Internet Age," Millennials have been raised to not only embrace the Internet, but to demand the Internet. We can't imagine life without it. According to a survey conducted by information technology research and advisory firm Gartner, 46% of Millennials between the ages of 18 to 24 said they would prefer having internet access over having a car. Are you still unsure about the Internet being the most impactful technological development in human history? What high school kid in previous generations would have traded the freedom of a car in exchange for sitting in the house with mom and dad all weekend?

Having access to information at your finger tips is the most widely viewed benefit of the Internet, but as it pertains to Generation Y, there are key benefits that many Millennials aren't maximizing or aren't even fully aware of.

Education

The future of education will live and breathe on the Internet. I'm not just talking about eCourses provided by colleges. I'm talking about grades K - 12 and beyond. Every year, school districts across America face budget shortfalls and in every Presidential election, education is a critical component of the conversation. I'm about to make some bold assumptions, predications, and declarations. Don't hold me to it, but don't be shocked if I'm right either.

What is the value of a teacher? What is the value of in-class instruction? Close to zero, and as time marches on, the perceived value of these two things will decrease more and more.

In the Internet Age, we now have streaming video, live chat, and high definition video conferencing. With all of this technology currently at our finger tips, why is it not fully being utilized? In the future it will be. It will be a long progression, but it will eventually happen. How do I know this? Because it's already happening in Corporate America. I've worked for major U.S. corporations in-house and externally as a consultant, and most of the people I've worked with I never met in-person, ever! If businesses are moving towards 100% remote working environments, why wouldn't our education system eventually fully adopt this system as well, especially considering that school is preparation for introduction into the workforce?

Classrooms will eventually disappear and be replaced in-home. As mom and dad work from home, the kiddos will be right alongside them learning from home. Teachers will still exist, but there will be far less of them necessary, as grading papers manually will become a thing of the past. This ancient process will eventually become 100% automated by computer programs, and not just with fill in the blank or multiple choice tests, but with digitally hand written assignments as well; assuming that human beings will be writing in the future and won't be fully converted to typing only. Teachers will eventually only exist as private tutors or instructors paid to teach via recorded video lessons that will be licensed to school districts nationwide as the accepted core teaching standard.

Yes ladies and gentlemen, this is the future of education in the Information Age.

So now that you understand the future of education, how can you benefit from this knowledge and capitalize on educational advancements taking place via the Internet today?

The first thing you need to do is understand the necessary

skills required for the present and future job market. When I was 18 years old in 2004 I was a bit of a visionary. I saw the future of the world. Smart phones didn't exist yet and tablets didn't exist either. Streaming video was barely stable and none of the technological luxuries we have today were even thought of. However, I knew that the day was coming when these advancements would exist. I paid attention to the trend line. I self taught myself business, traditional marketing and advertising, online marketing, web design, basic web development and coding, and I learned the Adobe Creative Suite. Throughout the last nine years, I've been continually re-educating myself on the latest and greatest in all of the fields previously mentioned. Learning these skills is what has allowed me to reach the level of professional success and opportunity I have achieved thus far.

Besides the ease and mobility of learning online, the most powerful benefit it provides you is the power to get ahead and stay ahead.

When I was a kid, my parent's required me to read literature and take additional math lessons over the summer prior to my next school year in order to get ahead. This helped me tremendously. By the time the new school year began, I was always ahead of the other kids. I've taken this lesson I learned as a child and have applied it to my education as an adult.

As you know from reading Chapter 1, I'm a college dropout. I dropped out of college not because I was incapable of doing the work or wasn't "college material". I dropped out because I realized after my Freshmen year that the institution of higher learning we have in America today doesn't allow you to continue your education, and you're falsely led to believe that there is a stopping point in your educational career. I don't care if you get an associates, bachelors, masters, or doctorate degree, you should never stop learning. College falsely leads you to believe otherwise. Traditional higher education also leads you to believe that you can "major" in one particular field and be completely inept in everything else.

The greatest decision I've made in the last nine years that has allowed me to thrive is continually assessing new skills required in the marketplace and then making sure I developed those skills. As it stands today I'm a professional marketer, but I'm also an intermediately skilled photographer, graphic designer, web developer, video editor, and copywriter. I learned all of these skills on my own through the Internet. I could have easily stayed in college to obtain a marketing degree to obtain the professional level marketing knowledge required to obtain job/business opportunities within the marketing field. However, getting a marketing degree doesn't come with the other skills I've obtained. It would have literally taken me decades to learn everything I've learned in the past nine years in a traditional college setting.

Before I go any further, I want to make it perfectly clear that I am not discouraging college. In fact, I believe that there's tremendous personal and professional growth you can achieve by going to college. I am simply making you aware of what worked for me and most importantly the present and future requirements in the job market.

There's a reason why recent college graduates with fancy MBA's can't find jobs. Although prospect employers won't tell them, the reality is that they lack the full skill set required to speak the language in today's modern business world.

I don't care what industry you're in, in today's world you will wear a minimum of three different hats and will therefore be required to know more than your college degree has taught you. If you want a job in marketing, but don't understand the lingo surrounding information technology, graphic design, and multimedia, you are headed for trouble. Don't worry though, it's not too late for you, and here's what I would suggest you or anyone with or without a college degree do to obtain additional skills for the modern workforce:

Lynda.com: I love this website. It's a subscription-based service currently priced at $25/month. By the time I had dedicated years and years self teaching myself 85% of

34 | What Next?

what I know today, I finally stumbled upon Lynda.com. Lynda.com has professionally produced video courses for everything including: web development, programming, business, marketing, photography, animation, and so much more.

If I could be in middle school, high school, or college all over again today, I would take every ounce of spare time I had on holidays, summer breaks, and weekends taking every single course available on this website. I taught myself 3D animation in 30 days using Lynda.com to create a promotional video for a business project. The results were amazing!

Here is the true beauty, essence, and benefits of Internet education... It allows you to learn at your own pace and it allows you to quickly and easily build your skill set which ultimately adds thousands and thousands of dollars to your earning potential.

Just imagine walking into a job interview with not just an MBA on your resume', but an MBA with additional skills in accounting, online marketing, animation, graphic design, and programming. You will easily add an additional $10,000 or more to your earning potential immediately! So many people waste so much time complaining about low wages as if they deserve to get paid more just because they sat in their seat a few years longer than the person sitting next to them. Seniority no longer matters and fancy degrees don't either. What matters today and on into the future is the additional benefits and value you can add to your position. Make yourself more valuable and you will see your income rise. There is no easier, cheaper, and more effective way to continue your education than online, and by online I do not mean an overpriced for-profit school. Save your money. I don't want to name drop and throw any particular schools under the bus, but those for-profit schools that spend millions of dollars convincing you to get into thousands of dollars of debt for another piece of paper aren't even respected by employers. What matters is not where or how you obtained your skills. What matters is that you have them. Sites like Lynda.com and others that are similar provide you with all of the tools you need to accelerate your skills and maximize your earning potential.

Social Networking

What is social networking? That depends on who you ask. Ask a 28-year old Millennial and they may say using Linkedin is social networking. Ask a 15-year old Millennial and they will likely say using Facebook or Twitter is social networking.

Social networking is so powerful when done right. It's

just a shame that most Millennials don't understand the true benefits of social networking or how to use it for professional purposes. Stalking ex-girlfriends and boyfriends and trolling your friends' pictures and status updates isn't social networking. That's not even socializing. That's just weird, but we're all guilty of it.

Social networking should be used just the way it sounds. Network with people socially. Facebook makes this difficult because it's a closed network, meaning you can't socialize with people you're not friends with. Linkedin is good, but you have to pay a monthly membership fee to maximize its full benefits. Plus Linkedin is primarily targeted towards an older audience. However, Linkedin is still hugely beneficial especially in the context of a professional social network. If you want to maximize your social network for job, career, and business opportunities Linkedin is king! So many people are confused about how to use Linkedin. It's really quite simple. The basic purpose of Linkedin is to connect with people whom you know on a personal and/or professional level. These people could be co-workers, colleagues, managers, former employers, etc. Once you've connected with these key individuals, stay in touch and watch the content they post through their feeds just as you would on Facebook or Twitter. The true magic and value of Linkedin as a professional social network is that it is a digital Rolodex of people you can take with you for life and reach out to in your time of need. So say you've connected with everyone you've ever worked with in the past on

Linkedin, then imagine one day you lose your job. Go to Linkedin, let your network of professionals know you're back on the market, and see what opportunities come your way. Since these people know you on a professional level and know your work ethic and skillset, they will gladly vouch for you and send you opportunities that they are aware of. There are also community-oriented benefits of Linkedin that allow you to position yourself as an authority in your respective field which can lead to business and job opportunities.

As much as I love Linkedin, it's geared towards a professional niche and is also a closed network, which disables you from connecting with people you don't know but would like to get to know. This is why Twitter in my experience is by far the greatest example of a true all-around social networking platform. Twitter is a 100% free open network so you can communicate with people without having to verify that you know them like you do with Linkedin or Facebook. Twitter is also geared towards all age groups. You can find any demographic you're looking to connect with on Twitter.

38 | What Next?

So how do you use Twitter or any other social networking site for professional use?

1. Establish a list of influencers within your industry or field of interest.
2. Follow, friend, and subscribe to every social network they're apart of.
3. Listen for updates in their social feeds and respond accordingly.

What does this do and what is the purpose?

Before asking that question, really think about the three steps I just outlined. These three steps are the exact same things you do with people whom you're friends with in the real world. In the real world you have a list of friends whose social networks you follow, friend, or subscribe to, you listen for updates when they post new things and you respond accordingly. Do you get anything valuable out of this exchange in communication? Sure, you might continue to build upon your relationships by staying in constant contact, but does this "social networking" provide you with job opportunities, business opportunities, or opportunities in general? Probably not. Unless of course, you're friends on Facebook with Mark Zuckerberg or Larry Page.

I've done exactly what I've outlined above. I've developed a list of influencers in the industries and fields of interest I enjoy such as business, marketing, and technology. I've been in constant contact with many of these people for so long that I've grown a very powerful relationship with many of them. So say I need some advice on getting this book featured in a prominent business magazine, I have a few people I can go to that can either directly help me get featured or at least help point me in the right direction. This is valuable information I can get from these people that my "real world" friends can't provide.

There is one thing that is extremely important about the power of this form of social networking. It MUST be authentic. Don't go make a laundry list of celebrities and think you're going to get Ashton Kutcher to start tweeting you back and forth and don't kiss people's behinds just because they're an editor of a major publication and your sole plan is to use them for your own personal gain. Authenticity is what the Internet really lacks. We are all a bunch of phonies. On Facebook we're all beautiful, slim and trim, and non-crazy. In the real world most people don't even come close to those levels of perfection. So be real! Especially when it comes to social networking. Influential people within the social media space can smell a rat a mile away and they have their defense mechanisms up at all times.

Here's another important thing to remember, social networking isn't a numbers game. It means nothing to have a large following if your followers aren't actively communicating with you. So don't go and join Twitter and go on a 10,000 person following frenzy. I'm only currently following a couple hundred people and I have only a little over 400 people following me back. These numbers by shear volume perspective aren't even close to impressive, yet I have established and continue to establish a very effective dialog with people I follow as well as those who follow me back. Many of the relationships I develop through social networking later turn into conversations taken off the social networking platform and carry over in other more connected channels such as email, phone, etc. This is when you know you've really built a powerful network.

Think about what you want to do in the future or are currently doing now rather it be your career or things you're interested in, and go follow and social network with those people in your field. The relationships you build will be invaluable in the long run. You will skate through life never having to worry about the lack of opportunity, because you'll always have a network that has your back.

I often like to equate social networking (when done right as I've outlined) to fraternities and sororities 2.0. Fraternities and sororities used to be the quintessential way to establish a global network of people you could always count on when you needed a helping hand in career advancement or job opportunities. Nowadays (for the most part) fraternities and sororities have become nothing more than an excuse to party hard.

The biggest problem with this reduced value in fraternities and sororities is that the business community no longer respects them and in many instances it reduces opportunity for many college grads looking to enter the workforce. When employers see fraternity or sorority on an applicant's resume' they often times draw the conclusion that that person is a partier who isn't serious and can't be taken seriously. Then you also have the issue of your prospect employer potentially being a part of a rival fraternity or sorority. It just opens up a huge can of worms, so tread lightly. My perception of fraternities and sororities by employers isn't just my assumptions. These are perspectives provided to me by former managers and business colleagues.

All in all, in my experience, social networking has been far more effective in providing me opportunity than anything else comparable such as a fraternity. Social networking (as a result of the Internet) allows regular people to communicate with people in their industry who are influential, thought leaders, and movers and shakers. Try finding these people in your fraternity or sorority. You might. But chances are you'll just find other people like you who aren't yet influential and don't yet have any valuable resources or opportunities to provide. I hate to beat up on fraternities and sororities, but I'm just providing a compare and contrast based on what's worked for me with social networking and what hasn't worked for peers of mine who went the fraternity/sorority route. The choice is yours.

As much as I love social networking, one enormous problem is fragmentation. Do you remember Myspace? That depends on how old or young of a Millennial you are. Myspace was one of the original social networking platforms. Where is it now? In the history books. It seems like there's always a new kid on the block in the social space. In the last seven years Facebook, Twitter, and Linkedin popped up and are now the Big Three. Now Instagram, Pinterest, Google Plus, Tumblr, and Path are on the rise. If there's one thing about social networking that troubles me it's finding a way to manage my activity on all of these platforms. Connect.com is fulfilling this need by bringing your social networks to one central hub to make the most out of the relationships you already have. Working as a social media manager and consultant for small, medium, and Fortune 500 businesses, I've seen how overwhelmed businesses get with the idea of prioritizing quantity over quality. Regular people have the tendency to do the same thing. They approach social networking like it's an arms race or a popularity contest to gather the highest quantity of friends and followers, but what about the quality of these relationships? Creating meaningful relationships through your social channels is the most important element of social networking. Without quality relationships, status updates, posts, Tweets, and pics will go unnoticed and unengaged. Build meaningful relationships, stay engaged, and watch your social channels work for you!

Real World Networking

Nothing will ever take the place of a real world face to face relationship. It's the easiest and quickest way to gain someone's trust. You could spend three months trying to get an industry influencer to respond to your Tweet on Twitter whom you don't know personally or haven't met in person. This is when real world networking becomes vitally important. I'm putting this section in the Internet Age Chapter because the Internet is a great source for finding real world networking events.

Sites like Meetup.com are fantastic for this. Six months ago I found a local Meet up group in my area called Startup Grind. Every week the group gets together and a prominent business leader takes the stage to discuss their start up journey. At these events I get to shake hands, meet, and exchange business cards with everyone from business investors to regular people just like me who are launching startups.

They say "birds of the same feather flock together." Start attending networking events and find people like yourself who have common interests. When I look at friends I grew up with there were some who stuck with friends from high school that were bad influences. This ended up bringing them down. Then there were people like myself who broke away from the pack and started to find people who were like-minded. Just because you have fun with someone doesn't mean that is the person or type of person you should be consuming all of your time with. Be able to find the balance and know the difference between your "drinking partners" and your "business partners." Walk with your drinking partners and fly with your business partners. You can find people to fly with at networking events.

Here's an additional tactic you can use to really take real word networking to the next level; expand your networking boundary nationwide or even globally if you can afford to do so. In today's day and age we truly live in a global economy. So go outside of your area and find networking events across the globe. The more people you know in more places, the greater ability you will have to meet more people who can help provide you with opportunities. Eventually you will be able to pay it forward and have a network established that you can use to help others. Imagine how gratifying of a feeling that would be.

If you're going to attend networking events in other areas, look for conferences. This is how you can get a chance to shake hands and meet big time power players. So say for example you go to a tech conference and social media guru and business mogul Gary Vaynerchuk is doing the keynote. After the conference (if you have an opportunity) introduce yourself to Gary and shake his hand. Don't expect to have a full-fledged conversation though. You're not the only person in the room who wants to meet Gary Vaynerchuk. The idea here is to get face time. After you've gotten face time, then you can follow Gary on Twitter and tweet him something like this:

Just met and chatted it up w/ @Garyvee at SXSW. He's such a cool dude.

Once Gary see's this Tweet he will instantly connect with it more than if you were just some random person on Twitter @ mentioning him.

If you get nothing else out of this two-part section on social networking and real world networking understand this... Human beings have a natural desire to connect with one another. It's what we do. When you authentically and genuinely connect with other people, they will eventually reciprocate. Not because they feel pressured to do so, but because they want to and because it's apart of their natural human desire. The more people of value you connect with, the more opportunities you will have and be able to pass on to others.

Building a Business

Never before in human history has it ever been as easy to learn and build a business as it is today as a result of the Internet. I am living proof of this. When I was in college I took an introduction to small business course. It was a joke and a complete waste of my time. The information was outdated and it was simply worthless, not to say that all business courses are like that; however, what took me an entire semester to learn about small business in a college course, I could have learned online in one weekend! That's the power of the Internet.

I believe with every bone in my body that the Millennial Generation will have no choice but to be entrepreneurial. I'm only going to briefly touch on this subject now because it will be discussed in more depth in a future chapter. However, I must say something about this subject briefly here since it's relevant.

The deck is stacked against us in terms of financial security. Having two incomes in the household is no longer good enough. We will eventually have to have four household incomes. Two from the jobs of both adults in the household and two additional income sources from side businesses each of the two adults in the household maintain.

If we were living in 1950 or even 1990 I wouldn't be able to say that building two businesses is easy or even possible. Nowadays as a result of the Internet Age, it is easy and it is possible to build a business and supplement or completely replace your job income. When I say easy, I don't mean get rich quick. What I should really say is easier. Easier than building a traditional brick and mortar business.

Building a business online simply requires the following:

- A great product with demand or desire
- A passionate business owner
- A strong desire to succeed

On that note, let's transition into the most important part of this 3-step equation: Passion.

Turning Passion into Profit

I will not spend a lot of time explaining how to build a business in this book as it really deserves an entirely separate book all to itself. However, I want to plant the seed for you to begin thinking about building a business by focusing on something you're passionate about.

Millions of people have supplemented or replaced their job incomes entirely by developing great products that they sell on sites like Etsy, allowing them to earn a full-time living. Tens of thousands of people are also earning a living blogging and vlogging about everything from politics to makeup tips through ad revenue splits from sites like YouTube. In both of these scenarios, selling products on Etsy and developing content on a blog or vlog doesn't cost a dime in marketing or advertising. It simply requires passion and the time taken developing content/products.

What's most important to understand about building a business is not the pursuit of financial riches. Building a business teaches you how money, personal finance, and marketing works, and it also allows you to understand how the corporate world thinks about money, employment, expenses, etc. If you understand business, you will understand how the entire world operates. Even if you fail at building a business (and odds are you will) you will at least gain the knowledge and understanding I just mentioned. This is what's most important. This knowledge and experience is invaluable and it can't be taught. It must be experienced.

Chapter 3: High School

Class Is IN Session

Time to get Serious

High school is where it all begins. This is where life begins to get serious. If you're in high school or you've already graduated from high school and you haven't begun to get serious about life and begin making decisions for your future, then you're already out in the world at a disadvantage. If you've already graduated from high school and are well into your college years or beyond and have already begun your career, it is still worth your while to read this chapter and put some or all of the following elements into action.

When I was in high school, like most kids, I wasn't exactly sure yet what I wanted to do with the rest of my life. However, I had a pretty good idea that I was going to be involved in business. I wasn't sure what level of business I would be involved in, rather it was marketing, executive level leadership or entrepreneurship. I just knew that I wanted to be involved in business. The day-to-day challenge of running a business and the creative component of developing a product or service and bringing it to market always excited me. It was part of my DNA. My mother's father was an IBM executive in the 80s, my father's parents are small business owners as were a few aunts and uncles of mine, and my parent's also had a few entrepreneurial endeavors. As you can see, business and entrepreneurship is in my blood.

Some people may read this and think I have an extra advantage because my path and destiny was very up close and personal, as I had numerous examples of successful people in my family who I could go to or be inspired by. While I definitely may have had an advantage as a result of my background, I never sought nor received business lessons or instruction by any of my family members. I consciously and subconsciously did the following activities. These activities made a tremendous impact on not only my ability to succeed within my chosen path in life, but it also gave me an even bigger benefit. I gained a deep level of understanding about myself, the world around me, and how I fit into it.

I don't care if you're in middle school, high school, college, or your career, everyone at any part of their life can benefit from participating in the following activities. The biggest benefit comes when you do them earlier but as they say, "better late than never."

Exploration

I believe in every fiber of my body that most people know what they want to do with their life as children. If they themselves don't necessarily know as a child, I believe adults around them know rather they be parents, teachers, or other adult-figures. When I say, "know what they want to do with their life," I'm not necessarily talking about the exact job or even the career they will choose as adults. I'm thinking more along the lines of aptitude. Your aptitude is your natural ability to do something. Our education system rarely gives children general aptitude tests and even when they do, they aren't administered regularly throughout children's school career. No wonder 80% of college students change their college major three times and no wonder the average person changes jobs seven to ten times in their lifetime. When you go through the most critical parts of your life as a child without exploring your aptitude, there should be no surprise why we get out into the real world and have no idea what we want to do with our lives.

Given the fact that every person has an aptitude that dictates certain characteristics that line up with certain professions; if you hone in on your aptitude at an early age and monitor your changes as you get older and on into high school, you will be able to greatly increase your likelihood of choosing the appropriate career path the first time as opposed to the second, third, fourth, or fifth time. This also ensures you have a greater likelihood of achieving happiness and prosperity throughout the course of your life.

Our factory-oriented education system that spits out 3,000,000 clones every year fresh out of high school is ridiculously flawed. The best example of an aptitude test we provide students across the board is the SAT (Scholastic

Aptitude Test). The SAT tests how well prepared you are for college level academics. What about a standardized test that gives high school students an indication about career choices best suited for them based on their general aptitude? I've never seen this test in high school? Did you?

Here's the unfortunate and sad news, a general aptitude test that becomes as standard as the SAT that is provided to kids from elementary school all the way through high school will likely never exist and be administered as a standard. So it is up to you to do this on your own. This is the part where parents who may be reading this book really need to listen up.

Earlier I mentioned my aptitude for entrepreneurship and business as a result of my DNA. What traits do your children have that you can identify that best line up with a specific career path?

It may sound like I'm making a mountain out of a molehill with this whole discussion about aptitude and it may sound like choosing what you want to be when you grow up is simply based on figuring out what interests you. I believe that is simply not good enough. The reality of life and jobs is that you rarely get to do what you enjoy, which is why according to a Yahoo Finance/Parade Magazine study, 59% of Americans surveyed have reported job dissatisfaction.

When you get out into the real world and start your first real job, you will likely find that it's not all fun and games and it's not the dream job you were promised by your high school or college guidance counselor.

Here's the other big problem that may hopefully help put this aptitude discussion into better perspective. Most high school and college students start thinking about their career based on what they like to do, then somewhere along the lines of misguidance from parents or other authority figures, high school and college students change their career path into fields that are "in high demand" or "pay well." I believe this misguidance is the contributing factor to constant college Major changes, career changes, and high rates of job dissatisfaction. High school and college students are trained to seek money as opposed to happiness. When you get out into the real world, you will find that high wages don't always equal happiness and in most cases they only equate to longer work hours, less personal time, more stress, and more pressure. I'm not saying that money isn't important. It's very important, especially when you live in a capitalist society. Somewhere between doing what you enjoy and doing something that pays well lies a sweet spot. When you know your aptitude, you can find this sweet spot easier and faster, and before you invest thousands of dollars seeking the wrong college degree and years pursuing a career you're dissatisfied with.

So here's the moral of the story... Live your life and choose your destiny for yourself. Dig deep inside of yourself as early in life as possible and pay attention to your aptitude. Constantly analyze and explore yourself and figure out the things that you are naturally good at and pursue those and only those things. This is how you will achieve happiness. It may or may not make you rich, but it will make you happy, and once you enter the real world, you will find that happiness is more important than any amount of money.

Extracurricular

Ever since I was a little kid, I remember it being ingrained in children and parents to involve children in as many extracurricular activities as possible. These activities typically included soccer, baseball, basketball, competitive cheerleading, hockey, or gymnastics. Do you see anything wrong with this list? I do. Every single extracurricular activity is a sport. I love sports just as much as the next guy, but why are we raising and glorifying kids who participate in sports, especially given the fact that so much time is dedicated to simply playing games. Couple that with the fact that less than 2% of college athletes go pro. To make matters worse, most kids who play sports are pushed into it by their parents, because their parents want to experience the joys of being a soccer Mom or Dad while sitting on the sidelines cheering on their kids. I'm not a parent yet, so I can't speak too ill of the feelings and desires parents have for their children's sports-related extracurricular activities; however, just because it may be customary and feel good to throw your kids into sports doesn't make it the right thing to do.

Extracurricular activities provide your child with a more well-rounded and positive life experience. In addition, it also gives them something constructive to do.

Instead of spending countless hours every week playing sports, what if you spent time learning a foreign language. What if after learning that foreign language you traveled to the country that speaks the language you learned, and you embrace the culture and speak amongst the natives? Wouldn't that be a better way to spend your time and money? Wouldn't that have more of a practical application on your life as an adult? Now imagine filling out a job application and you can say you're fluent in over four languages? Imagine how many extra thousands of dollars will be added to your salary. Imagine how much more respect and admiration you will gain from prospect employers, and imagine how many more opportunities you will have in life. In today's day and age with software programs like Rosetta Stone, there's absolutely no reason why you can't learn a foreign language by teaching yourself. It's much easier, faster, and effective than the watered-down foreign language classes taught in school.

Learning a foreign language is just one of many examples of outside the box extracurricular activities you can spend your time on that are more valuable long-term when compared to time spent kicking around balls. You could and should even take a lesson from the previous section about aptitude. Focus on your aptitude and allow that to guide you into other more productive extracurricular activities. If you enjoy theater and stage plays, take a trip to New York and go see Broadway shows. If you enjoy fashion, purchase every fashion book you can find plus a sewing machine and teach yourself how to design and create clothing. I could go on and on with more and more examples, but I think you get the picture. If spending money on these extracurricular activities isn't within your parents' financial means, then get a job and pay for it yourself.

Every child is not suitable to play sports and most kids aren't even good at sports, which is why stats prove that only 2% of college athletes go pro, and that's not even including the percentage of pro athletes when compared to the number of people who played sports as children that never even made it to collegiate level sports. That percentage would be incredibly low. Before you decide to take the time or continue to take the time to pursue extracurricular activities that don't and won't benefit your life long-term, think twice about other more productive ways you can spend your time that will yield a greater likelihood of positively impacting your future and your career.

Volunteering

Volunteering is so important. Without volunteering as a young person, I'm not sure you can ever truly become a level-headed human being. Volunteering requires sacrifice, emotional investment, and a sense of humility. It also allows Millennials to shed a few layers of selfishness.

When I was in high school, I was involved in a program called P.A.L. (Peer Assistance and Leadership Skills). Our responsibility was to be leaders in our school, our district, and our community. One of the programs we were involved in was mentoring underprivileged and disadvantaged children from a neighboring elementary school. I remember being assigned to mentor a first grade boy. For the sake of his privacy, I'll keep his name confidential and refer to him as James. James was a quiet, disconnected, but very smart young boy who unfortunately came from an abusive home. While mentoring James an hour per week, we would play board games, read books, hang out, and just chit chat. Being a mentor to James was one of the best experiences I had in high school. It allowed me to gain a sense of reality and a deeper perspective of life in the shoes of another person from a different background. James may have felt that he learned a lot from me, but I learned far more from James. I gained a better understanding of life outside of my bubble and it allowed me to become closer with myself.

Volunteering at children's hospitals, nursing homes, elementary schools, veterinary clinics, Veterans hospitals, or anywhere else you can is an experience that will stick with you for the rest of your life. You'll feel better about yourself and you'll take lessons learned that you can apply to the rest of your life.

More than any other time in your life, I believe that volunteering should begin in high school. Maybe even middle school. When you're in high school, your body is going through intense feelings and hormonal imbalances, and you're beginning to shape your identity. Why not throw in something really positive like volunteering to make sure you balance some of the bad stuff like narcissism and selfishness.

Internships

Internships are often only perceived as activities you partake in once you get to college and are well into your junior or senior year. That is way too late. If you begin interning in high school, you can get a head start on solidifying what you really want to do and what you really don't want to do with your life.

Say for example your whole life from grade school on into college you thought you wanted to be a lawyer. Once you get into your sophomore or junior year of college you finally decide to do an internship at a law firm only to realize you hate the long hours and you hate pushing around papers all day. How much of a bummer would it be to have your career dreams crushed at 20 years old? This scenario could be prevented if you had interned at a law office during the summer of your sophomore year in high school.

I never did a traditional internship when I was in high school. However, I did something a little more advanced. My mother is a Realtor, and on weekends while in high school I would occasionally go with my mom to show houses. As a result of this experience, I got an in-depth look into self-employment, how the home buying process works, and how sales works at 16 years old. This has had a huge impact on my life. What 16 year old kid knows how the home buying process works? None I know.

If an internship isn't necessarily something you can do because of the industry you want to be in, consider simply going to work with your parents for a day to get an in-depth look into life in the corporate world or whatever world they are working in. It may make you think twice about pursuing or not pursuing a particular career path. You may go into the office with one of your parents one day, see what they do and be bored out of your mind. If you can't imagine sitting solitary in a desk for 8 - 12 hours per day at 16, that feeling will not change when you're 26 either, trust me.

I hope I've been able to give you insight into some things you need to consider while in high school. I've done these things and they've positively impacted my life substantially. If you do these things, they will have a profound affect on your life as well.

The ultimate thing to remember here is to get a head start. Don't wait until college or even worse, wait after college to do these things. They should be done at the high school level if at all possible.

Chapter 4: Higher Education

CLASS OF 20??

Skills to Pay the Bills

What comes to mind when you hear the phrase higher education? You may have keywords pop in your mind such as necessity, requirement, must have, etc. When I think about higher education what comes to my mind is: Is it worth it? How much debt will I incur? What is the value?

If those aren't the things that come to mind when you think about higher education, you may need to reassess your mind. Higher education and a university degree in many ways doesn't hold the value it used to. On one hand, a college degree is more necessary now than ever before and on the other hand, a college degree is more worthless now than ever before.

In this chapter I aim to set the record straight on higher education for Millennials. The ultimate value of college will depend purely on you, your circumstances, and your career path. If you plan on being a doctor, then college is not only necessary it is an absolute requirement. However, if you plan on being involved in business, marketing, the arts, or any other related fields, I would argue that not only is college unnecessary, it may very well be a complete waste of time and money.

Is College Right For You?

Is college right for you? This is the first question you should be asking yourself before diving head first into a 4 - 6 year commitment with tens of thousands of dollars of debt. Most high school students who come from upper middle class families with high GPA's are automatically programmed to believe that attending a college university is the default step right after high school. Before you make this decision be sure to weigh all of your options.

When I graduated from high school I was pre-programmed to go straight into college. I chose to start out attending a community college. The cost of tuition and books was 70% less than a major university and the quality of education was highly accredited. Accreditation is the one caveat that is extremely important. If you don't live in an area with an accredited community college, then it isn't worth your time or money attending. I checked with the University I planned on attending after community college to ensure my credits would transfer over. After they verified that all of my credits would transfer over, my decision was solidified. I worked full-time the summer before my freshmen year of college and was able to pay for my entire freshmen year of community college leaving me with zero debt and zero student loans.

Going straight into a university after high school sounds fun, and I'm sure it is with the freedom away from parents and the taste of adulthood. What more could you ask for? Before you run off and pursue the high life, consider these statistics:

- Approximately 35% of students who enter college will drop out during their freshmen year.
  (Source: Brighthub.com)
- Only 63% of students who enroll in a four-year university will earn a degree, and it will take them an average of six years to do so.
  (Source: The Education Trust)
- 37% of students will either drop out of college before finishing or flunk out of their programs of study.
  (Source: USA Today)

Do you see how high the odds are that you will not only enter a four-year university and not graduate, but it is also more likely than not that your four-year degree will take an additional two years to complete? This means two additional years of room and board, textbooks, and college tuition. Are you willing to risk tens of thousands of dollars given the odds?

I don't want to sound like I'm discouraging college

just because odds are most students (like me) will not graduate. I'm simply giving you a reality check to bring you down from the social high you may experience as a result of parental pressure, social pressure, and internal programming you've been trained to believe since grade school.

My biggest concern I have for Millennials is that we are entering universities by default. Most people are not college material and don't have a firm grasp on what they want to do with their lives, yet they start off their adult lives with thousands of dollars of debt.

I can talk about student loan debt and give metaphors for how terrible it is all day long, but why don't I just shoot it straight and give you a realistic example of how big of an impact student loans will have on your life.

According to a recent study conducted by the Project on Student Debt, a student advocacy organization, the average monthly student loan payment in 2006 was $242.82 paid over the course of ten years. Other estimates for today's average monthly student loan payment show twice that amount. For those of you not living in the real world yet, this means you will have to sacrifice lesser living conditions for up to ten years of your life after college. An additional $250 - $500 monthly bill could and likely will require you to live at home for several years after college, drive a beater for several years, and/or live in a crummy apartment for several years. You will experience this lack of luxury until your student loans are paid off and until you begin to receive better job offers and raises, but don't look forward to that happening until you're at least five years into your career and are in your late 20's early 30's.

There is a very simple solution to this financial crisis.

Option 1: Live at home, attend community college, work fulltime, and transfer to a local university after completion of community college. This will allow you to pay for college as you go and graduate debt free.

Option 2: Attend a four-year university straight out of high school and live at home until you graduate. If you work full-time throughout your entire college years and don't spend money frivolously, you should be able to graduate debt free or come pretty close to it.

Where most college students go wrong from what I've seen from my peers, is that they immediately leave the nest after high school, attend a four-year university, and they don't work. This formula is a recipe for financial disaster. It allows for too many outgoing expenditures with no income to pay for them.

In addition to figuring out how you're going to finance your college education, you need to also determine if college is right for you. You may be best suited to attend a trade school, take time off from school to explore yourself and your passions, enter the workforce directly and work your way up, or pursue entrepreneurship.

When I graduated from high school I chose all of the above (minus trade school) and it worked out extremely well for me.

One very important thing you need to also consider is time. I spent a lot of time in this section discussing the high financial cost of a college education. You may attend college; get all the way to your senior year and dropout, subsequently leaving you with thousands of dollars of debt without even receiving your degree. You may even graduate, but have loads of student loan debt. One thing I can tell you from my life experience thus far is that I've gone through thousands and thousands of dollars exploring life. Exploring life is what you're really doing post-high school. It doesn't matter if you're working retail, going to college, building a business, or backpacking in Europe. The sole purpose of your life post-high school and on into your 20s is to explore life and really hone in on your passion and figure out what you want to do with the rest of your life. Since graduating from high school in 2004, I have wasted thousands of dollars exploring life, but one thing I never wasted was time. You can always make more money, but you can never make more time. Once time is gone it's gone.

Before you make any major life decisions after high school, be sure you put several days, weeks, or months into your plan. The last thing you want to do is wake up, be 30 years old and realize you wasted your time and you have nothing to show for it.

Even if you graduate from college, are 30, and still have mounds of student loan debt, at least you can say you spent time completing your college education.

Life is short, and your 20s will fly by faster than you can imagine. What you do in those ten short years will likely dictate the outlook on the rest of your entire life. So if you remember nothing else I've mentioned thus far, remember to use your time wisely. Figure out what you want to do with your life, map out a plan to get there, and go for it!

Antiquated Education

College is expensive and the cost of a college education rises more and more every year. The cost of a college education isn't the only thing you should be concerned about though. Our entire education system including higher education is tremendously antiquated. Ever since I can remember, the education system has been behind the times. Look at technology and the classroom today? Students are still issued big expensive text books costing school districts $200 plus per textbook. Why not strike a deal with these book publishers and make all textbooks on all grade levels in eBook format, and instead of giving students eight $200 a piece textbooks, why not issue them eReaders instead? This would immediately bring down the cost of local and federal education expenditures. Why is this not happening? One likely reason is that textbook publishers are trying to milk school districts for as much money as they can as long as they can. The other more likely reason is that the people who are in power that run our education system are behind the times. They are too lazy, too uninformed, or too uneducated about modern technology. This epidemic is just one of many examples that illustrate how antiquated our education system is, and it's the reason why trade school attendance is on the rise.

Let's say you want to gain higher education to become an artist or a graphic designer. Should you choose a major university or a trade school? If it were me, I would choose a trade school. You will get more in-depth and specialized training at a school geared solely towards art as opposed to a traditional all-encompassing college program. Now for those of you who are esteemed advocates of a traditional college education based on its ability to make you a more well-rounded individual, I would request that you take a look at the world you live in today. No longer is the world smothered with a bunch of round individuals. The world (led by Millennials) is increasingly becoming populated with square pegs that simply will not fit in round holes, and oddly enough this isn't what employers want anyway. An employer would much prefer someone who has a more specialized education and skill set as opposed to someone who has a general studies degree or a traditional marketing degree in a world where traditional marketing is soon to be largely dominated by online marketing. A college graduate who gets a marketing degree today will have learned little to nothing about online marketing, and what they did learn one year prior will be obsolete on the day of their graduation.

Let me give you some insight into how this applies in the real world. In the real world, employers (to a large degree) no longer care about where you received your experience or your skills. They just want to know that you have the skills, the experience, and can perform on the job. If that means you should go to a trade school as opposed to a traditional university to get the best education, then go to a trade school. Sure, it might sound sexier to say that you graduated from a major university as opposed to a trade school, but if you gain better training, knowledge, and skills that later transform into higher paying opportunities from a trade school program, you win!

Don't ever let society tell you what is best. The greatest people on Earth, who have accomplished the most, did so by achieving things through unconventional methods.

Now before you run off and go enroll in a trade school, be extra careful to do your due diligence. The trade school enterprise over the past decade has become littered with overpriced schools that deliver sub-par education. So do your homework.

The main point I want to drive home here is that you must think outside the box. If you choose a career field that a traditional university only has watered down programs for, then consider another option.

One of the main reasons I dropped out of college is because no college on the planet offered Internet marketing classes or degree options in 2004 and most still don't today, despite the tremendous rise of search engine marketing, pay-per-click advertising, and social media marketing. This is yet another example of how antiquated the traditional education system is.

Unfortunately for our current education model, the world simply moves too fast, and the institutions of higher learning can not and will not ever be able to adapt to the modern needs of business. This is why so many Millennials are running the world nowadays. There are literally thousands of Millennials out there just like me. Just like Mark Zuckerberg, Steve Jobs, Bill Gates, and other young savvy individuals who self-taught themselves vital skills that the modern institution of education simply couldn't teach them or didn't have programs for early enough.

Textbooks, old school marketing programs, and libraries. These are just three of many examples that prove our education systems' antiquation.

I believe it is vitally important you be made aware of this as you head out into the real world and determine how you will gain skills to be a productive adult. College may be the path for you, but it could also be a trade school, on the job training, or trial and error entrepreneurship.

The True Value of a College Education

I've spent this entire chapter thus far being hyper critical about college and the value of a college education or lack there of. This is the part where I dial it back a bit.

I've written this book primarily based upon my life experiences. Sections in this book that are not based on my life experiences are based upon the experiences of my peers as well as widespread experiences I've found through research. Since so much of this book and my recommendations are commentary based upon my experiences, I also realize that everybody is not me, and as such everyone doesn't have the skill, desire, or aptitude to take on the world without a college degree and walk out successful in their own right.

Let me make one thing perfectly clear as it pertains to higher education... For the typical Millennial, it is absolutely necessary. Even when I think about myself, the lack of a college degree will eventually result in me hitting a career ceiling. I may continue to climb the ranks of upper-level management, but it is likely (due to corporate politics) that I will never rise to the ranks of executive level leadership as a result of me lacking a college degree. That level of leadership is oftentimes filled with "good ol boys" who will only allow people to play in the sandbox that are similar to them. ie: college graduates. I can't say I don't blame them. It's human nature for people to surround themselves with people who are just like them. Thankfully for me, when I dropped out of college, I did so knowing these implications and I prepared myself for my destiny of entrepreneurship.

When you're an entrepreneur, you can have the fanciest degree or have no degree at all. It doesn't matter when you're the boss.

Hitting a career ceiling is one big reason why I would advise every Millennial pursuing a career as an employee to get some form of higher education from an accredited institution; rather it's a university or trade school. It helps you get your foot in the door.

One thing that is vitally important you understand about the value of an education is that it is only one part of a multi-step equation. In addition to having a college degree, you also need to have charisma, charm, passion, and an on-going evolution of experience. The world isn't what it used to be. With every generation, there become more and more college graduates. The simple economics of this equation spell bad news for Millennials without higher education. There is an excess supply of college graduates and not enough jobs to fill them all with employment opportunities. This allows the ball to be completely placed in the business communities' court. I believe this is one of many reasons why pay raises have flat-lined for decades. I also believe this is why so many college graduates are often times being offered low-wage entry level jobs after college, when those jobs traditionally were filled by the uneducated.

The world we live in today requires you to step your game up more than ever before. When I was 18, I realized that I could learn the skill set required to become a professional in my career field faster and more effectively by teaching myself the necessary skills I needed. So that's exactly what

I did. Before you choose to pursue or not pursue higher education, ask yourself if you can obtain the necessary skills required for you to succeed with or without a college degree. Allow the answer to this question to help guide you down the right path.

Life in the real world today, especially for Millennials requires you to be remarkable. I've said it before and I'll say it again and again. It is no longer good enough to succeed in life just being average. In addition to higher education, you must be a leader and an influencer. I've used the word higher education in this chapter over and over and have often times equated it to college. Higher education isn't just an adjective for college. It's an adjective for higher learning. Learning that evolves after grade school. In your life you will always be learning and you should always strive to gain even more knowledge and skills to truly perfect your craft and skill set. I gained my "higher education" in the school of hard knocks through self-teaching and trial and error. You have multiple paths to choose from in the pursuit of higher education. Make sure you choose wisely.

Chapter 5: Build a Brand

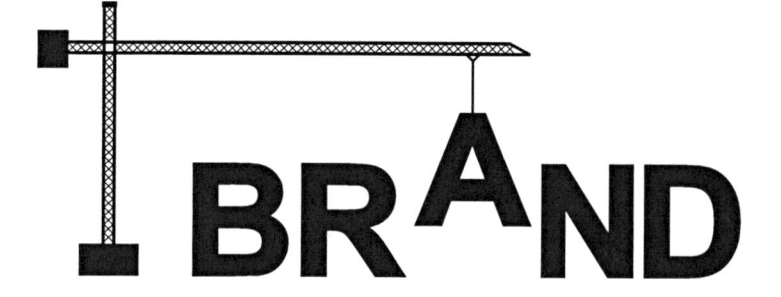

Be Somebody

What comes to mind when you think about P.Diddy? Entertainment and party extraordinaire. What comes to mind when you think about Donald Trump? Real estate mogul. These are personal brands and they used to be limited exclusively to celebrities and professional athletes. Not anymore. Thanks to the Internet, blog platforms, and social media, building a personal brand is now possible for anyone despite their lack of celebrity status. Hundreds and soon to be thousands of people are building personal brands using social media platforms, blogs and vlogs.

No one is more poised to have the technical understanding to build a personal brand through online tools as well as Millennials. Building a personal brand is vitally important. It goes along with my reoccurring theme of being remarkable. It's that extra step that 99% of people won't take. When you take the initiative to build a personal brand you separate yourself from the rest of the pack of average people who aim to get their foot in the door purely with their college degree and lack luster resume'.

In this chapter I will tell you exactly what I've done to build a personal brand as a social commentator and digital media marketer. I'm no Seth Godin, Gary Vaynerchuk, or Perez Hilton, (not yet at least) but I have been able to successfully build an online presence that has given me credibility which has led to phenomenal job and business opportunities.

Start a Blog

In the beginning, blogging was primarily only utilized by geeks and teenage girls. They were initially and primarily used as an online diary, but later transformed into the standard for online news organizations and the backend technology for most websites. In laymen's terms, a blog is nothing more than a website structure that allows for quick and easy archiving of new content that is displayed to the end user in chronological order as new content is posted. This is very different from traditional websites, which typically don't rely on frequently updated content.

In 2010 I started a blog that I updated daily with my commentary on current events. I wrote about everything from politics, to technology, to digital marketing, to funny pictures and videos. I had a lot of big viral moments where some posts would reach 100 – 2,000+ social shares with dozens of comments. Creating and maintaining this blog allowed me to further solidify my skill set within the social media and content creation and management space, which has directly led to the opportunities I've gained within the last three years.

I love social commentary, which is why I decided to start writing books. Writing a book was the next logical progression for me as a blogger. Now you may be thinking to yourself that you don't have anything interesting to say or you may even hate writing. I understand. Most people don't like writing and most people aren't good at it, but that's the beauty of blogging. It isn't a contest of writing ability. With a blog, it's about captivating an audience with compelling content that provokes thought, entertains, educates, and/or engages; simply re-posting a funny cat picture followed by one line of commentary counts as blogging.

When developing a blog for your personal brand, develop content based on your passion and your career field. If you want to be a lawyer, develop a blog with on-going content about juicy high-profile public lawsuits. State the news and facts, and then provide your commentary. If you want to be a doctor, develop content based on new advances in the medical community. I think you get the point. Since (in these two examples) you would be focusing on current events, there will be lots of people searching the Internet for this type of content. As your blog grows in age and content quantity, your blog posts (web pages) will eventually begin to get indexed in search engines based on the related keywords within your blog posts. This is how you will gain free traffic to your blog through search engines.

Building a blog with content related to the industry within your field gives you an advantage over others you're competing with in your career field for job or business-related opportunities. It shows that you are tremendously serious and passionate about your career field. I started my blog at 23. If I could do it all over again and if the technology was available, I would have started a blog in high school. If you're in high school or college, I would encourage you to start there as well. This will allow you time to build years and years of content, which will further solidify your commitment to your career field in the eyes of prospect employers or others you seek an opportunity from.

Now that you're aware of the benefits of starting a blog, you might also want to know how to actually build a blog. The first thing you need to understand is the differences in the types of blogs.

There are two different types of blogs: Hosted and un-hosted. Hosted blogs require you to purchase a domain name (ex: yourblog.com) as well as a hosting package. A domain name has an annual cost of approximately $15 per year depending on the domain name registrar you choose. A hosting package has a monthly cost of approximately $10 - $20 per month depending on the hosting provider you choose. If you don't want to pay for a blog you can create one for free as an un-hosted blog using a platform like Wordpress.com or Blogger.com. The downfall of creating an un-hosted (free) blog is that you're severely limited in certain customization options such as the design, analytics, and add-on (plugins) options. In addition, many un-hosted blogging platforms don't allow you to use your own custom domain name, and in exchange you're required to use a sub domain of the platform you host with such as yourblog.wordpress.com. This looks very unprofessional, the URL is too long for people to remember, and it makes it blatantly obvious that you were too cheap to pay for your blog.

If you decide to take the plunge and develop a hosted blog, you will have several blog platforms, domain registrars, and hosting companies to choose from. I use Wordpress as my blog platform. I purchased my domain from Go Daddy, and I host with Hostgator. In the last paragraph I mentioned Wordpress.com as an un-hosted blogging platform. This is true. However, you can also download the Wordpress blog platform (software) and install it on your website allowing you to reap the benefits of Wordpress's robust platform plus the unlimited control and customization benefits of self-hosting.

If everything I'm saying is beginning to sound like Greek don't worry. It's really not that complicated. Here's the process I took in setting up my blog:

1. Purchase domain name (GoDaddy.com)
2. Purchase hosting package (Hostgator.com)
3. Install Wordpress using a one-click install option within

the Hostgator control panel

If you're still confused, do some Google searches for: "How to setup a Wordpress blog" or contact a web hosting company for additional support. Once you go through the process you will see how super simple it is.

I hope by now after reading this section you understand the power and importance of building a blog for personal branding purposes. This is just the beginning. The true essence of building a personal brand requires that you gain a following, and this is where social networking and social media come into play.

Social Networking

Social networking and social media allow us to connect on a global scale, and it also allows information to exchange hands and flow to others extremely quickly. Building a social network of followers who interact with you from a brand perspective is incredibly powerful! Just imagine building a blog in high school or college and two or three years later after consistent posting, you begin to average thousands of site visitors to your site every day and thousands of people following you on Facebook and Twitter. Do you have any idea how powerful that is? Here's some perspective:

Kim Kardashian has been reported to earn an estimated $10,000 per Twitter Tweet when endorsing a product or brand. This is purely as a result of her 17 million and growing Twitter following. Odds are you will not be gaining 17 million Twitter followers anytime soon (if ever). However, the point I'm illustrating is the value of a social network to a public figure (personal brand). In Hollywood 1 million Twitter followers will automatically have big businesses calling to pay you per Tweet. In the real world, simply posting frequent content to your blog and growing a couple hundred or couple thousand person social media following will yield you a raised eyebrow because it's so unusual and outside of the box. It also signifies that you have other people who believe in you and embrace what you have to say. Its social proof at its finest! When a prospect employer sees that you have an industry-specific blog, you post regularly, and you have a hundred or more social media followers who tune in to hear what you the "FILL IN YOUR INDUSTRY HERE" expert have to say, it instantly gives you credibility in the eyes of the employer or person you're seeking an opportunity from. Think about it. How many people can say they have 100 or more people who tune in regularly to hear what they have to say about something serious outside of your personal social network of friends and family? Not many.

As you grow your blog content and you place links on your blog to your social networks, over time you will organically gain a social media following. As your social media following grows, regularly update your social networks with updates of links to your latest blog posts. This will keep your fans and followers coming back for more, and you'll begin to develop an even larger more engaged audience.

Develop a Portfolio

A portfolio of your work is essential, and not just a tangible manila folder filled with pieces of paper. I'm more specifically referring to an online portfolio. I have an online portfolio that features every accomplishment I've ever had in my career. It's laid out like an extended visual resume'. Employers and business prospects love this! Put the URL to your online portfolio on the top of your resume' that's posted online and simply watch how many more businesses contact you with job offers. It works. It just simply works! The same rules of setting up a blog apply here. So If I were you I would setup your online portfolio as a hosted Wordpress blog and look for portfolio themes. The theme is the look and feel and design of your blog. This will allow you to have a professional site that's easy to navigate and easy to develop. You can find free and premium Wordpress themes by doing a simple Google search: "Wordpress themes." After you've found a theme you would like to use, simply download the theme to your computer and use the one-click install feature within your Wordpress dashboard.

In addition to showcasing career accomplishments, also be sure to include details about any degree's or specialized training you've received, a link to your blog, a list of companies you may have interned for and the work you did for them, community service work, references from teachers, professors, mentors, managers etc. If you're currently in high school or college and you lack work experience, building your online portfolio now will allow you to begin thinking about the previously mentioned action items to cross off your to-do list to later be included in your portfolio once you've accomplished them.

The goal and purpose of your online portfolio is to be a virtual sales tool. Employers who are scouring resumes' on job posting sites are looking for people who stand out. When they come across a resume' that has a link to a website portfolio visually laid out with accomplishments and achievements, your resume' will instantly rise to the top of the stack!

Work for Free

Yep! I said that. Work for free. Working for free to gain experience is also more commonly referred to as interning. Interning often times becomes a watered-down process whereby you get paid minimum wage to sit at a desk and file papers all day. That is not at all what I'm talking about.

I'm talking about gaining real experience. Experience you can put on your resume' and having those skills gained be applied to future jobs or career opportunities.

From the time I was 18 to 21 I did tons of free work for family, friends, and clients. I did this so that I could build my experience and skill set. On the client side, it provided me opportunities to later up sell and get paid for other services. The beauty and magic of working for free is that there's no way you can lose. Sure, you're doing work without compensation and are therefore sacrificing loss of time, but look at the guaranteed upside. The guaranteed upside is that you gain experience, plus if you do a good job odds are the people or businesses you do free work for will eventually hire you or pay you for future projects, and/or they'll refer you to others.

Don't ever miss an opportunity to work for free. Here's another secret and additional add-on tactic. Shoot for the stars and contact the most prominent companies you can find in your industry, and ask them flat out if you can work on a project with them for free to gain experience. When you say the words, "work for free," their eyes will light up and they'll likely be more than willing to give you an opportunity. After all, there's nothing for them to lose. You will then add this experience to your resume' and your online portfolio. Rinse and repeat this process over and over again and you'll wake up 1 – 2 years later with a ton of work experience with prominent companies making you a true commodity within your industry.

Are you beginning to see how this personal branding process all comes together? Are you beginning to see the value and benefit? Building a personal brand isn't about becoming the next A-list celebrity or top 100 blogger, although if you stick with it you very well might become the next Internet celebrity/guru. Building a personal brand is about becoming an expert in your field and providing social proof along the way to illustrate to people within your industry that you are the real deal. You're not just another guy or gal who got an MBA and now feels entitled for the world to lay out the red carpet for them. When you put in the sweat equity and build a brand, you become a serious figure that others look to with respect and admiration.

Years ago I realized that my only real competition in life was myself. The average person is extremely lazy and unwilling to think outside the box or put in extra work. How many other 27-year olds take the time and money to self-publish their own book? Not many. I did.

When you think outside the box and take extra steps to become remarkable, you will have a lifetime of success and prosperity. So go out there. Start a blog. Build a social network. Develop a portfolio and work for free. I promise you it will pay off. I know this because I've done it and the results have been astounding! Best part is… I'm just getting started!

Chapter 6:

Surviving Corporate America

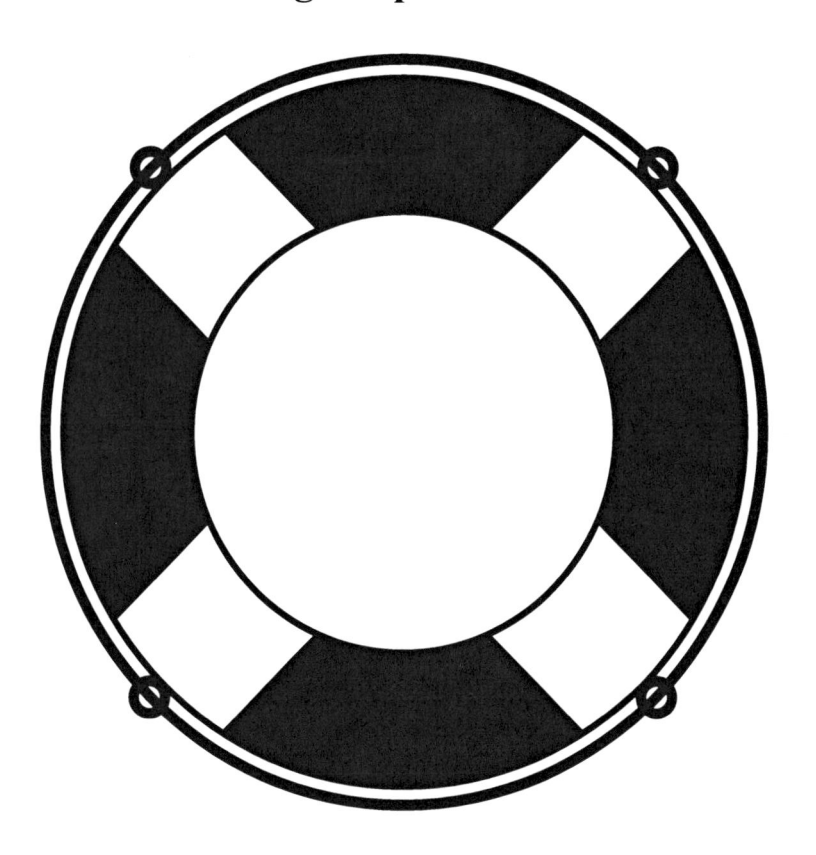

Survival of the Fittest

The corporate gig. It's the shining beacon of success for many people, especially college graduates. Landing a desk job in Corporate America for a Fortune 500 Company is what dreams are made of. I've been there and done that. I've even worked for a Fortune 10 company. Working for a huge corporation can be both cut-throat and compelling all at the same time. Not everybody will work for a huge corporation, but no matter what size company you work for rather it be small, medium, or large, there's some things you need to know to survive if you plan on climbing your way to the top.

Millennials possess certain key traits that are detrimental to surviving in Corporate America. In understanding this, I felt it extremely important to dedicate this chapter as a guide of pitfalls to avoid, things to understand, and things to be aware of before entering Corporate America or any professional job for that matter.

When I entered the corporate environment I was totally lost. I was unaware of how to navigate corporate politics and I found it difficult to deal with the ridiculousness of seniority, whereby people who sat in their desk for ten or twenty years longer than me got an increased say so despite their inexperience in a particular field I had more experience in. I also just couldn't understand why upper management didn't see things my way. After working for numerous companies of all sizes throughout the last eight years as a consultant, contractor, and in-house employee, I've experienced Corporate America on many different levels. Hopefully you can take from my experiences and make your entry into Corporate America more smoothly, and if you're already in Corporate America, you can still learn a thing or two from reading this chapter as well.

I've broken this chapter down into bite-sized zero-fluff life lessons. Read, enjoy, and perhaps even learn a thing or two.

Know Your Role

Dwayne "The Rock" Johnson. He's an A-list actor now. Fourteen years ago he was a championship wrestler in the WWE. He was my idol. Part of his routine was to tell his opponents this rather catchy line in an attempt to put them in their place.

"Know your role and shut your mouth!"

I think that line illustrates the perfect mindset you need to have upon entry into Corporate America. No matter where you are in life, no matter how old you are, and no matter how much power or status you have, you will always have someone else above you or lateral to you that has the power to check and balance you. "Knowing your role" isn't about being walked on and stepped over. It's about being humble enough to realize that everybody above you once stood in your shoes, and as you climb the ladder, you too will one day gain power, respect, and admiration.

Know Your Worth

Knowing your role as I suggested in the last section will not only reduce your heart rate and prevent you from getting unnecessarily angry when things don't go your way, but it will also keep you humble and level-headed. Being humble and level-headed is one thing. Being marginalized is another. Often time's businesses and managers will do everything in their power to marginalize young people, especially if you're passionate, talented, and possesses certain skills or leadership abilities that your manager does not. Beware of jobs and managers that try to reduce the importance of your role, title, or influence. They will do this to keep you convinced that you deserve less pay, a lack of recognition, diminishing or non-existent pay raises, and a low level title. If you find yourself in this position head for the hills and run away as fast as you can! If you're in this situation and you lack job experience and that's what you're there to gain, that is one thing. However, after you've passed the point at which you've paid your dues, don't allow yourself to be taken advantage of. I'm not suggesting that you storm into your managers' office after one or two years and demand a raise. I'm saying, look at the climate within your company and find out where you stand. I suggest going to your manager after you've passed the two year point of proving yourself and ask him or her how you're doing and what future you have with the company. If he or she gives you an uncertain answer, then this is your cue to begin looking for a new job.

When you're out in the real world prospect employers will judge the decisions you've made in your career, and if they see on your resume' that you held a position with high levels of responsibility but were paid low wages, they will question why you stayed at that job for a lengthy time without receiving adequate compensation or an appropriate title based on your lengthy responsibilities. This issue calls into question the legitimacy of your resume' or even worse it can make a hiring manager feel entitled to screw you over the way your last employer did. It's a vicious cycle. As an example, say you're a scheduling coordinator for an auditing company and you coordinate everything your company does including coordinating events, schedules, audits, and perhaps you yourself are even audited to ensure you're doing your job correctly according to industry guidelines. That's pretty stressful right? Your manager may try to convince you that you're nothing more than an office admin. That is a lie! You are a project coordinator and could pursue employment elsewhere making much more than you make in your current position, especially if you're getting office admin pay for doing project coordinator duties.

Employers will do everything in their power to keep you marginalized so they can reap the benefits of giving you less than you deserve. Be mindful of this and always know your worth. With every job you have, determine your skills and responsibilities and compare and contrast them to other jobs and careers in your industry. See where you line up as far as years of experience and compensation. Sites like salary.com offer free tools to allow you to do this research in a matter of minutes! Doing this research periodically is also a great way to ensure your skill set matches up with the needs businesses have in your industry, ensuring that you never fall behind the curve.

So many people both young and old go through life at dead end jobs simply because they've been led by their managers to believe that's all they're worth. What are you worth? If you don't know find out. Your future depends on it!

Get in Good

Have you ever watched the television series Survivor? That show created a reality TV phenomenon of alliances, whereby contestants would align themselves with others for the sole purpose of advancing their position in the game. Corporate America is a game. Yep, I said that. In this game there are winners and losers. Those who win get in good with their managers, their managers' manager, and they climb as high as they can to get in good with as many people as they can. This is vitally important for the purpose of self-preservation and career advancement. When you're on your mission to get in good I wouldn't recommend doing anything disingenuous or making yourself look like an obvious suck-up.

Getting in good involves attending every company function, getting to know as many people as possible, and engaging them on not only a professional level, but a personal level as well. It's a fact that people buy things from people they know, like, and trust. You are selling yourself and people will buy you if you get to know them. This will eventually lead to them trusting and liking you. This will really come in handy when the finance department starts making budget cuts and layoffs. If someone is looking at laying off a few people and you're on a list of a hundred others, but you've "gotten in good," you just may be spared the rod.

Be Valuable

How can you add value to your position and to your

company? This is a question you need to be asking yourself regularly. Adding value will help you rise as an asset. The first thing you can do to immediately begin being more valuable is to figure out what you can do to make your manager and co-workers jobs easier. On the job, everybody's overworked and underpaid and nothing brightens someone's day more than having their load lightened. So offer up yourself to do some heavy lifting to lessen the load for others on your team. Striving to be more and more valuable is the best and easiest way to gain job security. The essence of being valuable is simply making yourself indispensable. Become so valuable that your manager just simply can't live without you, and watch as raises, advancements, and lack of termination come your way.

Nights and Weekends

Long hours. This was by far, the hardest thing for me to deal with and accept when I entered Corporate America. For some reason no one ever told me that 9 - 5's no longer existed. 5 (A.M.) - 9 (P.M.) is the new 9 - 5. Prepare to come in early, leave late, and maybe on occasion even put in some extra hours on the weekend. If you're not cut out for long hours because you "have a life," then Corporate America is not the place for you.

Leadership

Up until now, I've spoken a lot about being subordinate. Being subordinate has its place, but you also need to spread your wings and become a leader. You will never rise above the ranks if you're stuck being somebody's #2. Understand though that leadership isn't necessarily about calling the shots and you don't have to be a manager to lead. You can demonstrate leadership by leading yourself. Be reliable. Be dependable and even be outspoken. When you're called on in company meetings to give your opinion, speak up, speak clearly, and speak like a leader would speak. Ever since I was a kid, I've always been intrigued by speech. After high school, I began reading business biographies of famous business leaders. To take it a step further, I also began listening and watching interviews of people like Steve Jobs, Warren Buffet, Donald Trump, Gary Vaynerchuk, and others. The power these great leaders possess when they speak immediately commands respect and attention. Pablo Picasso once said, "good artists borrow, great artists steal." Go find business leaders you admire and steal their style, mannerisms, and gestures, until you develop your own style.

Bring People Together

Division is the greatest problem that plagues Corporate America. There are so many egos and so many departments that often times people don't communicate properly. This leads to a failure of accomplishments and it stifles progress. Even though this issue exists and everyone knows it exists you will be hard pressed to find a leader rise up and bring people together. Why don't you become that leader to bring departments together? This may sound like a David vs. Goliath feat to accomplish or you may feel that it's above your pay grade, but it's really not and just because you're not the boss doesn't mean you can't do it.

Dysfunction within the corporate environment doesn't happen because of a lack of care or concern. Dysfunction happens because there's a lack of competent and compassionate leadership. Often times management and executives get so caught up in hitting their numbers that they allow flow and structure to fall by the wayside. If you want to bring an entire company together, go talk to every senior manager in every department you deal with and ask them how you can better work with them. Once you've assessed their needs, then you can formulate a plan that aligns with everyone's objectives. Your hard work will not go unnoticed. Bringing people together directly increases productivity which leads to increased revenue.

When the big guy or gal in charge sees revenue go up, they will be able to directly attribute it to your hard work in bringing people together. You know what that means? Raise, bonus, promotion, and job security. There's one very important thing to keep in mind here. Make sure you let people know when meeting with them that you plan on bringing people together. You don't want your hard work to go unnoticed and you don't want someone else taking credit for it, so plant your stake in the ground, bring people together, and collect your reward.

Transparency

Transparency is how you maintain sanity. In a perfect world, you will work for a manager who allows you to be transparent, and they will also have an open door policy for you to express how you feel about anything without placing judgment against you. Transparency is really just another word for honesty, and if you can't be honest with people you work with I'd advise looking for a new job a.s.a.p. I'm not advocating job hopping. However, in this scenario the biggest problem with the lack of transparency is that it creates dishonesty and backstabbing, and this disease is contagious. It spreads like a plague, and you don't want to catch this virus and have it begin to affect the way you communicate with others.

Whiners vs. Winners

No one likes a whiner. They're annoying, loud, and they are perceived as being weak individuals. Millennials love to whine, because we're used to getting everything we want in life and most of the time we're used to getting things we didn't earn. Don't bring that mentality into Corporate America. Check that attitude at the door. Turn that frown upside down and transform yourself from a whiner into a winner. If something is bothering you, learn to separate real problems from exaggerated problems and ask yourself if you're building a mountain out of a mow hill. Odds are you are.

You may not have gotten the promotion or the credit you deserve, but just remember, you are new in your career and you are the low man on the totem pole. Your advancements, promotions, raises, and credit will come in due time. Often times I wonder if managers intentionally bully people as a means of testing their strength. If you get screwed over and your manager knows it, react like a winner and pretend it doesn't even affect you. Your manager will notice your strength and give you what you deserve the next time around.

One thing to remember is to not accept being treated like a doormat. Getting taken advantage of a few times is one thing, but be aware of a company culture in which this may be common place. If this becomes the situation, re-evaluate your position and its longevity accordingly.

Cut Throat

Cut throats and stabbed backs. Sometimes places of employment can easily lead to a murder scene. It's unfortunate, but be prepared to become a victim. It's just a part of the Corporate America initiation process. Like all things in life, it's not the situation that matters. It's the way you handle the situation that matters. In realizing that Corporate America can be a very cut-throat environment, be careful to maintain a high level of professionalism with your colleagues and don't make the dreaded mistake of befriending people without getting to know them for a long time. Making this mistake could cause you to become prey for a victimizer looking to size you up to make sure you don't rise above them. On the note of cut-throat, it's also important that I mention co-worker attitudes. If you work within a department of five or more, it is highly likely that at least one person within your department will be disgruntled and bitter about their position within the company. Watch out for these people. They will constantly speak negatively of the company as a whole and poison your mind with all sorts of nonsense which eventually leads you to hating your job. Don't allow a Debby Downer to dictate the experience you have on the job. Be self-aware and draw conclusions from your experiences as opposed to the experiences of others.

More Money More Problems

The more money you make the more problems you will have; when I say problems I'm referring to more responsibility, stress, pressure, and anxiety. It may sound great getting paid $50K or more at 25-years old, but realize that that dollar figure comes with a higher level of problems you will deal with. Employers will expect much more out of you, so don't think getting a raise to $50K or more is a reward. It's a recipe for harder work, which isn't necessarily a bad thing if you're prepared for it. Since I just informed you of this, consider yourself warned.

Interviewing

The interview process is so much more than just a Q and A session for the employer. What they really want is to engage with you. They want to ensure that you have the aptitude and ability to communicate on a professional level. They want to see how you think and react on the spot to questions you can't prepare for. An interview is more of a psych evaluation than anything else. I attribute my ability to have gained tremendous opportunities and salary advancements in my career thus far largely due to my ability to interview extremely well. I'm a true people person. I can size up a person in a split second and in doing so I immediately know how to communicate with them.

The most important component to an interview besides answering the prospect employers' questions appropriately is for you to ask thought-provoking questions. Ask your prospect manager about their personal life and what it is about their personality and career goals that made them a good fit for this job. Ask them real life questions about where the company is headed, what the turn-over rate is, etc. Getting a job is very serious, and you need to make sure you're taking a job with the right company. By asking the two questions I just suggested, you will get a strong sense of how valuable the company is to your potential manager and how much confidence they have in the company's future. It's vitally important that you know these types of details so that you can make an informed decision before hopping on board a company that may lay you off or close up shop in the next 90 days.

In addition to having outside the box interview questions prepared, make sure your demeanor mimics the interviewer. Slouch in your chair slightly, cross your leg, and have a pen and piece of paper ready to write down notes about their answers to your questions. You need to make them feel like they are on trial, just like they want you to feel. This balances the power dynamic which allows for a high level of mutual respect, which results in you getting hired. Another very important part of the interview process is due diligence. Due diligence is the research you do to ensure the company is solid. You can ask your prospect manager all sorts of questions about how solid the company is, and they will likely lie to you. In fact, it's likely they will lie to you about most aspects of your job, especially if they really want to hire you. They'll say whatever they have to say to close the deal. Be prepared to be lied to about hours of operation, the stability of the company, future growth, your job description, and just about everything else. If you're prepared to be lied to in the interview, it will make it easier to accept if you're hired and you decide to take the job and their lies become a reality.

Doing your own due diligence prior to the interview will also help you avoid simply taking their word for it. Thanks to the Internet and sites like Glassdoor.com and Indeed.com, you can find reviews and even salary information for many companies. This will help you separate fact from fiction by getting a perspective of the company and your exact position by hearing reviews from people who have already filled your shoes.

Contracting

Contracting. It's the unfortunate new reality of the job market and it's become widespread at companies of all sizes. Contracting positions can last anywhere from a month to a year and sometimes even longer. Sometimes employers will even tell you their position is contract-to-hire. Be aware that this could simply be a bait and switch in an attempt to make you feel like you may have a chance at getting a full-time salaried position.

If you're unfamiliar, contracted jobs come without any benefits. No employer-sponsored health insurance, time off for sick days, holidays, vacation, or paid time off, period. It's a real bummer. However, there is some upside. Contracted jobs are typically confined to a 40-hour work week which means after your eight hours are up each day, you're off the clock and on to enjoying your life, whereas salaried jobs require you to work until the job is completed which leads to long nights and weekends. The other benefit of contracting is that it is typically easier to get a job as a contractor since there's less risk for the employer. Contracting gives employers tremendous benefits. It's easier to terminate an employee with less paperwork, they don't have to pay employment taxes, and they don't have to pay benefits. As a result, employers will typically go through a less tedious vetting process when hiring.

Job vs. Career

Job vs. Career. Wow! I really wish someone would have explained this to me when I first entered Corporate America. It would have saved me a lot of unnecessary stress. In life, you will learn that there's a time for everything. This is especially true when it comes to establishing and understanding the difference between a job and a career. Some jobs will be pretty crappy. The hours may not be very flexible and management may not be very fair, but if you're gaining valuable experience you win in the end. Nothing in life is permanent, so realize that some jobs may be temporary placeholders that you may be forced to endure in order to gain experience, build your portfolio, and move on to bigger and better opportunities.

Employment vs. Entrepreneurship

After going through all of the pitfalls and guidance I've provided from lessons I've learned about life in Corporate America, I hope you've seen the upside and downside. Most importantly I hope you've been able to appropriately assess rather or not you're cut out for Corporate America. Not everyone is. I for one was not. However, I knew that before I could ever truly become a great businessman, I had to work for great businesses and I've had the opportunity to do that. Some people are natural born leaders. Corporate

America tends to stifle leadership, especially within young people. You're forced to sit in line and wait your turn, and your turn may not come for ten, twenty, or thirty years, if ever.

I'd love to speak more in-depth about the pursuit of entrepreneurship, but that would take an entire book. For all intents and purposes of this book you are reading now, just know what you're getting yourself into. Entrepreneurship can seem very glorious, especially in a day and age in which college drop-outs are creating multi-million and billion dollar websites and mobile apps in their college dorm room or their parent's basement. Entrepreneurship can be very glorious, but it's also hard work.

Millennials have lots of quirks that make us insubordinate, overly emotional know it all's. Oddly enough, these are all great characteristics that can be molded for entrepreneurship, because when added together these characteristics have the potential to develop into passionate leadership.

Millennials are a unique set of people. We grew up being democratized more than any other generation prior. We were born and bred to speak our minds and maintain passionate enthusiasm about our core beliefs. Although often viewed as a negative by older generations, I believe these traits will allow our generation to change the world in ways no other generation before us ever has, as these character traits align themselves with some of the key principles that define success.

Are you an employee or an entrepreneur? Before you answer this question, explore both worlds equally through research and even application and see where you end up. You just might be surprised. It has never been easier to learn and build a business than it is today. Even if you fail, the experience in building a business will change your life forever and allow you to better understand business, Corporate America, employment, and life in general. Building a business will test you in every way imaginable and show you what you're truly made of. It's a journey on a rollercoaster ride, but if done right the end result will be worth the bumps and bruises.

Chapter 7:

Escaping Corporate America

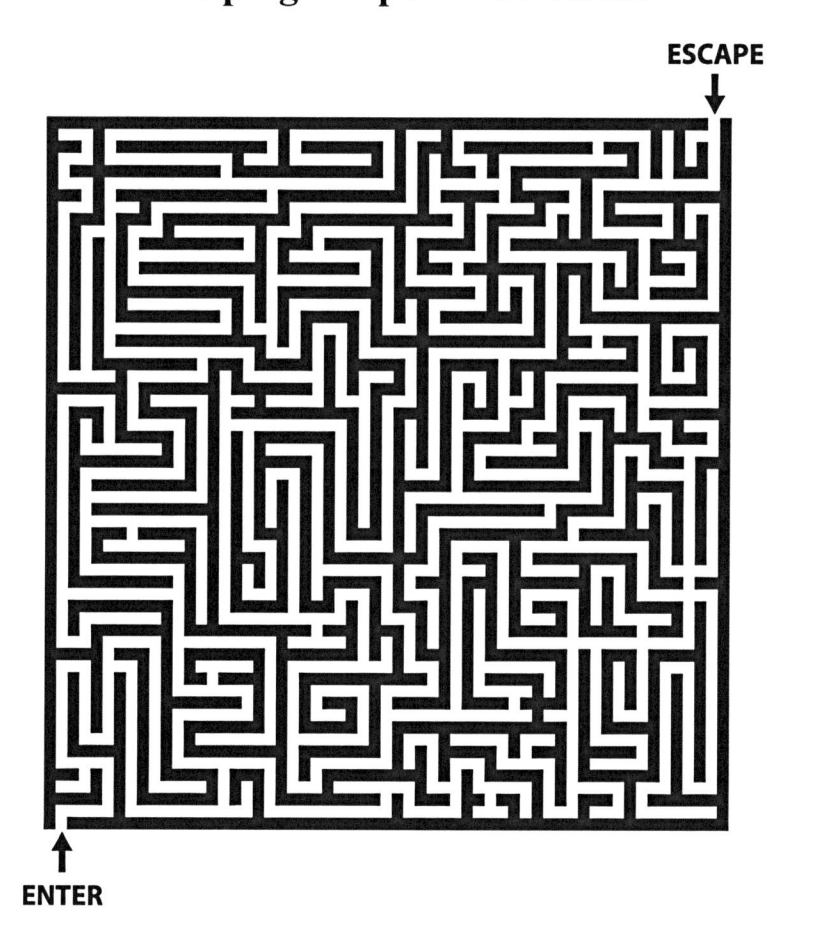

ESCAPE

ENTER

Run for Your Life

Have you entered Corporate America and discovered that it's just not right for you? Are you on your way into Corporate America and feel it's not right for you after reading through my last chapter? Have you begun to discover that your aptitude aligns more closely with Entrepreneurship as opposed to employment? If so, then this is the chapter for you. One thing I want to make perfectly clear before getting into this chapter is that entrepreneurship is not easy and employment is not necessarily terrible. Sometimes people who choose to escape Corporate America do so because they hate their job and they prematurely attribute their negative experience at one or a few jobs to be the experience they will have at all jobs. Then they run off and join some MLM pyramid scheme in hopes of finding a path to entrepreneurship. That is absolutely not the appropriate way to view employment or entrepreneurship. Entrepreneurship isn't for everyone and it shouldn't be your Plan B just because you hate your job. Entrepreneurship is also not a route you take simply because you think it's the easy way out or because you want to be your own boss.

Before you take the plunge into entrepreneurship, you really need to know what you're getting yourself into. I believe that entrepreneurs are primarily born, not made. Meaning, there are very few people who have the aptitude, patience, and skill for entrepreneurship naturally. However, that doesn't mean that entrepreneurship is outside of your reach just because you aren't gifted with the talent for business naturally. Entrepreneurship is definitely something that can be learned with hard work, perseverance, and determination. Entrepreneurship is more of a state of mind than anything else and it begins with leadership, passion, and creativity. In Chapter 4: High School I referenced the unfortunate side effects of what happens when students at early ages never take and continue not to take aptitude tests throughout their school career. If you look inside yourself and are on the fence about rather you should pursue employment or entrepreneurship, start by taking an aptitude test.

In the last chapter, I mentioned that I went into Corporate America to learn business at a high level. I was an entrepreneur before I landed my first corporate gig. However, understanding how the game is played from the top has given me more understanding of business than I ever could have learned through trial and error entrepreneurship. I say that to say, consider entering the workforce before you take on entrepreneurship. This is why I titled this chapter Escaping Corporate America as opposed to Skipping Corporate America. There is tremendous value in understanding how the game is played from the inside out, as opposed to making educated guesses based on case studies and trial and error-oriented decision making.

Business 101

I said it before and I'll say it over and over again. Entrepreneurship is very difficult. Before you take the plunge, you will first need to make sure you have three basic business essentials. They are as follows:

- Business idea you're passionate about
- Capable, dedicated, and skillful team
- Understanding of modern marketing

I could go on and on for days about more essentials you need to develop a successful business. However, I believe the preceding three bullet points to be the most important.

Since the age of 18 I've run all sorts of businesses. Some were successful, but most were complete and utter failures. I've developed a few profitable ecommerce sites and I even ran a marketing consultancy firm.

I will be the first to admit that I'm not the shining example of business success. Not yet at least, but I'm getting there. It's taken me over eight years of life experience running small business ventures and working in Corporate America to get to the point where I am today.

One side note of advice you should understand about business is to make sure you don't over complicate it. You don't have to be a millionaire or a billionaire to have a successful business. You simply need to provide a product or service that people are willing to pay for. Writing this book is a business. It's a product that I own that I am selling. In the traditional over-hyped sense of the word business or entrepreneurship, most authors don't consider themselves business men, business women or entrepreneurs, but they are.

You may like drawing stick figures with funny captions. Think that's not a business? It is. In fact, there's a guy who does this (iwanttodrawacatforyou.com) and he's extremely successful. He even got Billionaire investor and Dallas Mavericks Owner Mark Cuban to invest in his company.

I'm going out of my way to make a very important point here, which is to make you understand that a business simply starts with an idea you're passionate about. It doesn't matter if you make $1,000 or $1,000,000.

After developing an idea you're passionate about, you will need to find and surround yourself with people who have the skill set, capability, and dedication to help turn your idea into a business. These people will ideally have marketing skills, web development skills, and business acumen. You can find these people on Linkedin and at local meet ups on Meetup.com. You may even be able to find people on Craigslist.

After you've solidified your dream team, you will need to make sure you understand modern marketing. Modern marketing is different from traditional marketing whereby marketing messages are one-directional. Modern marketing incorporates interaction with your marketing messages. As an example, social media is a huge component to modern marketing.

Outside of Corporate America, I got my greatest education in business by reading a few key books. I'm not being compensated in anyway by recommending these books. These are books I've personally read and even re-read from time to time. These books have shaped most of what I know and understand about modern business and modern marketing. They are as follows:

- Think and Grow Rich: Napoleon Hill
- The Art of the Deal: Donald Trump
- Purple Cow: Seth Godin
- All Marketers are Liars: Seth Godin
- Crush It: Gary Vaynerchuk
- Rework: Jason Fried

In addition to these great books, Udemy.com and Mixergy.com are also great resources that feature tons of excellent interviews and crash courses that explain everything you need to know to build a business in today's modern market.

Savings

Spending money is great. Saving money is even greater. Saving money will be critical for your escape out of Corporate America and into entrepreneurship. A lot of so-called "business gurus" will try to convince you that you don't need money to start a business. This is sometimes true but generally false, and even if your business doesn't need a ton of money to launch, you still have personal expenses and bills to pay for.

One of the hardest challenges you will face when building a business is worrying about money. You do not want to be in this position. It is very scary. You also don't want to be building a business with the expectation that those earnings right off the bat will go towards funding your business growth and paying your personal bills. These two expenditures need to be kept separate which is why it's so important that you have an established savings fund. Ideally, you should have twelve months of emergency funds that will allow you to pay your personal expenses and bills should you decide to escape Corporate America and pursue your business fulltime. I'll be the first to admit that this is difficult which is why I advocate so strongly for saving money in your post-high school and college years. The last thing you want to do is create a bunch of unnecessary debt going to college and then find yourself post-college trying to build a business as well with mounds of student loans weighing you down.

In addition to your twelve month emergency fund, estimate how much it will likely cost to fund your business venture. Here are a few basic things to account for:

- Website development: domain name, monthly hosting, maintenance
- Marketing and advertising funds
- Devices: Computer, Internet service provider
- Office supplies: Pens, paper, printer ink
- Product development: Prototype, product inventory
- Freelance services: graphic designer, web designer, product designer

These expenses may sound very expensive and they are. Before you invest the money into some or all of the above, start small and prove the concept of your business first. There's nothing worse that can happen to an entrepreneur than wasting time and money building a product or service that nobody wants. Conduct a small focus group with friends and family, give an in-depth explanation of your idea, and ask them to give you feedback. If you can find ten people that are just as excited about your idea as you are, you might be on to something.

Risk

In the last section I ended by discussing how expensive building a business can be. Entrepreneurship is a huge risk and unless you are truly passionate about something, you won't be able to handle the risk or stick it out emotionally. Risking the loss of money as a result of a failed business is a very likely scenario. You should also realize the risk in time. When you begin building a business, you will find your life becoming totally consumed by it. It will begin to occupy your nights and weekends.

Understanding the risk of time and money as it pertains to entrepreneurship is something you need to get a firm grasp on. A lot of people will try to circumvent the money issue by taking on loads of credit cards to finance their business. This is a viable option that many entrepreneurs utilize to finance their business. Just realize that it is very dangerous and can often lead you to waste money on things you otherwise wouldn't have if it was your hard-earned cash you had to part with.

One of the things that have always pushed me to work harder pursuing my dreams as an entrepreneur is realizing just how short life is. Many people wait until their 30s and 40s to start businesses. In my opinion, this is the absolute worst time to ever start your first business. When you're in your 30s and 40s, most people generally have a family to take care of. I've heard countless amounts of horror stories of middle aged men and women who gamble everything they own to finance their business and pursue their dream, only to have it end in a nightmare.

The beauty of youth is that you get the chance to screw up a little, make bad decisions, and generally not have those decisions destroy your entire life. This isn't the case when you have a family who is depending on you to make less risky decisions to provide them with stability.

If you have even the slightest idea in your mind that you may want to start a business, do it now while you're young. Throwing away one, two, five, or even ten thousand dollars at 25 is nothing compared to throwing away that money at 40. That could be money that goes towards your mortgage payment or your children's college fund.

Life as an entrepreneur has its risks and its rewards. Make sure you are in the game at the right time and don't come in too late.

Plan

Having a solid plan is the key to limiting risk in any scenario in life. A plan helps keep you accountable. When sitting down to outline a plan for your business be sure you keep the following in mind:

- How much money do you need to fund your business?
- How long will it take you to fund your business?
- Have you established a 12-month emergency fund?
- Have you developed an idea you're truly passionate about?
- Have you secured the right people to help you bring your business to market?
- Do you understand how modern marketing works?
- If you leave your job to pursue your business, be sure to leave on good terms with a reference letter.
- What will you do if your business doesn't work out?
- How deeply will you be impacted financially if your business fails?

Developing a solid business plan will help ensure you're in the right frame of mind to take on the responsibility of building a business. Did you notice that the suggestions

I outlined for your business plan had nothing to do with sales projections, growth expectations, and other typical business plan terminology? That's because this stuff is virtually irrelevant to begin with. Instead of focusing so much time and energy worrying about the future, focus on the now and figure out the details of future business growth as the business grows. I've seen so many entrepreneurs (myself included) get stuck in what I call analysis paralysis. They waste a lot of time worrying about the future of the business one, two, five, and ten years from now. Then they look up six months later and see that they never started building the business. Don't become a victim of analysis paralysis. Like Nike says, "Just Do It!"

If entrepreneurship aligns with your skills and aptitude, give it a shot, especially while you're young. You just might develop the next big idea! Just know what you're getting yourself into.

Chapter 8: Financial Literacy

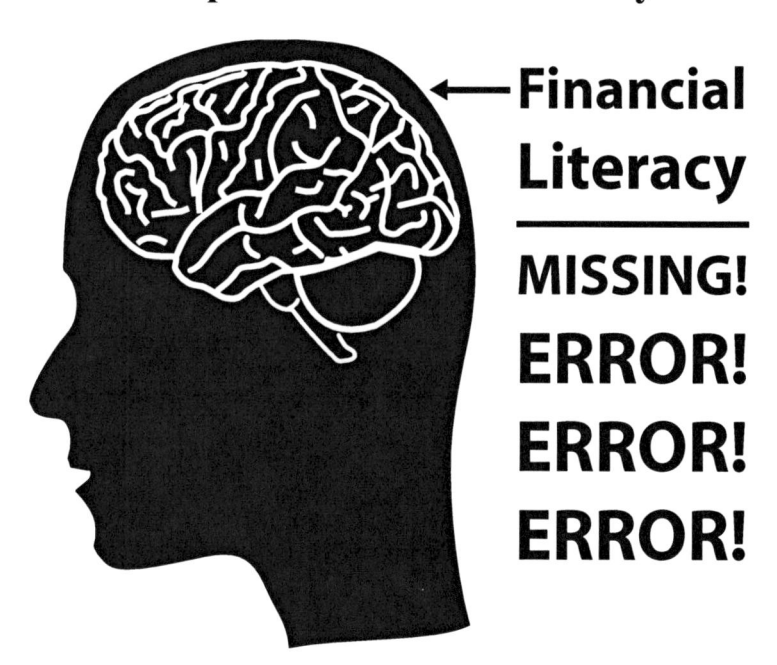

Financial Literacy ←

MISSING!
ERROR!
ERROR!
ERROR!

1 + 1 = Huh?

Were you taught how to balance a bank account in high school or college? Did you learn how to buy a car, buy a house, split bills between your spouse or significant other, or save for retirement? I sure wasn't taught any of this. Not by teachers or college professors. Why is this? Why are you required to take macro and micro economics classes in high school and college, yet you're never taught basic financial literacy? This is just another example of how antiquated and ineffective our education system is.

Before I begin giving financial advice, let me provide a huge disclaimer and state the following loud and clear:

I am in no shape or form a licensed financial advisor.

My suggestions are based on actual financial strategies I put to use in my personal life.

America is hopelessly and shamefully financially illiterate. Somewhere between the pursuit of happiness drafted in the Declaration of Independence in 1776 and modern America, we misconstrued the true meaning of The American Dream. Somehow the American Dream got twisted into what has become The American Nightmare. The unfortunate and saddest element of this disaster is the fact that people who are living the American Nightmare aren't even aware of it.

Check out these shocking and alarming statistics:

- Nearly half of Americans have less than $500 in savings. (Source: Huffingtonpost.com)
- Only 14% of American workers are confident they will have enough money to live comfortably in retirement. (Source: Employee Benefit Research Institute)
- Nearly 75% of retirees have not saved enough and said they would save more if they could do it all over again. (Source: uMich.edu)
- 56% of workers report that they have not attempted to calculate how much money they will need to have saved for a comfortable retirement. (Source: Employee Benefit Research Institute)
- 30% of Americans say they will need to work into their 80s to be comfortable in retirement. (Source: Usnews.com)
- 49% of Americans say they aren't contributing to any retirement plan. (Source: CNN.com)

Are you scared? You should be. This could be your life one day. You could end up becoming a statistic. Your life doesn't have to end up this way. I can't tell you how to invest for retirement, as I'm not a licensed financial advisor. However, if you consider using a few basic financial principles I outline in this chapter, you will be able to immediately gain a better grasp of financial literacy.

Preparation

Preparing for your financial future begins in high school; if not high school, then college. If not college, then you definitely need to begin planning right after. However, if you made the mistake of taking on loads of student loan debt in college, realize that you are already disadvantaged. That's ok though, as long as your career requires a college degree and you're passionate about your chosen career field. Nothing in life is free, including education, so if you have student loan debt, don't fret. Debt is a natural part of life and your college education could be a valuable investment in your career.

Much of what I'm about to go over has already been discussed in previous chapters. However, given the subject of this chapter I think this is a good place to provide a summary as well as additional detail that hasn't yet been discussed. As you know by now after reading this book up to this point, I didn't complete college. The financial advice I'm providing in regards to college was the financial plan I outlined for myself my freshmen year. This plan is common sense. However, sadly most things that are common sense aren't necessarily common.

High School:

1. Work part-time while in high school. Spend 25% and save the remaining 75%.

My dad taught me a savings lesson years ago that is incredibly applicable to high school students. He told me that whenever I get my paycheck to take 10% in cash and put it in a safe in my closet. Not a bank account, but a safe. Why a safe and not a bank account? When you put money in a safe every 1 - 2 weeks when you get your pay check, you visually see your money increase. It becomes tangible and it becomes a game in which you get excited to see just how high you can stack your money. With your remaining 90%, use 25% for discretionary spending and put the remaining 65% in a savings account. I must admit, I didn't do this in high school and I regret it.

As of today, the Federal minimum wage is $7.25 per hour. A high school student that works part-time should earn an average of $400 per month net. This would allow you to save $300 per month. That is only $200 less than the average American has in savings total, and you as a high school student could be saving that amount of money each month!

So let's continue to do the math. $300/month x 2 years (Junior & Senior year of high school) = $7,200 in savings!

College:

1. Attend community college your first two years. Average savings: $10,000. (Source: Usnews.com)

2. Live at home while in community college or your entire college years: Average savings: $32,000. (Source: Finance.Yahoo.com)

3. Work while in college. Live off of 50% and save the remaining 50% to pay off future student loans or pay for college as you go.

It can be very tempting to move away from home and live on campus or in a college dorm room to get the full college experience, but try to separate the allure of freedom for a better financial future. The money you will save living at home is enough to pay for a luxury automobile in cash or put down a hefty down payment on a house. What would you rather have? Four years of fun, a sweet ride paid for in cash, or a down payment on a house? Please choose wisely.

First Job Jitters

Your first real job! It sounds so exciting right? You put in the hard work in school. You kept up your grades, you graduated, and now you're living in the real world with your first real job. Congrats! Just don't get too excited just yet.

I don't want to doom and gloom you to death, but I do want you to realize that just because you made it to the party doesn't mean you've "arrived!" According to The Bureau of Labor and Statistics, the average person will have 7 - 10 jobs in their lifetime, and within those 7 - 10 jobs could be 7 - 10 totally different careers.

Your first job is not the time to go out and paint the town red. Don't go buy that cool new sports car or hot little VW Bug, and don't go out and rent a lavish luxury apartment because you think you deserve it. You don't deserve anything. You just got your first real job! At this point in your life and your career, you need to do the following:

- Pay off debt: credit cards and student loans
- Establish a 12 month emergency fund in the event of a job loss
- Determine satisfaction with your career choice

I could count on all ten fingers and beyond the amount of times I've heard adults say that your 20s are the best years of your life. They really aren't. It's not miserable and you should definitely have fun and enjoy your youth. However, when this message of "the best years of your life" is heard by young people, they equate this to mean time to goof off, get in debt, and take life less seriously. That equation could not be any further from the truth. When you look at the stats and see that half of American adults only have $500 of savings total, there's no surprise that adults and parents are misguiding an entire generation into believing your 20s is code word for "party time."

Your 20s is the time to hunker down and begin making responsible decisions. This includes changing the people you surround yourself with. You need to quickly remove people from your life who aren't a positive influence. This means ending relationships with negative people in the real world and un-friending negative friends in cyberspace on your social networks. The last thing you need is an irresponsible friend convincing you to quit your job and go backpacking in Europe when you've established a financial plan that you have obligated yourself to sticking to for your long-term benefit. After you've trimmed the weeds out of your life, paying off debt and saving money for your future is next. Weddings, cars, houses, and babies are very expensive and they don't necessarily come at the right time or in the right order. After college, you may still be driving your 10-year old hand-me-down from your parents. What happens when it breaks down? Can you afford to get it fixed or even worse, buy a whole new car?

Getting your first real job can be very exciting and you may feel like you've "made it." Be proud and be happy, just don't be overzealous in your spending.

Tracking Expenses

Tracking and monitoring your expenditures is the most critical component to staying accountable to your long-term financial plan. There are two ways I've approached tracking expenses. You can choose which one works best for you.

Option 1: Hardcore

If you are extremely attention-detailed, then "Hardcore" is the expense tracking option for you. This option relies on you tracking every single one of your expenses. It doesn't matter if it's a $.99 cheeseburger. Tracking every expense is the only sure fire way to know exactly how much money you're spending. After going "hardcore" and tracking every nickel and dime you spend, you may be shocked to see how much money you're wasting: $1 here, $10 dollars there. It all adds up and in the end and you could be wasting hundreds of dollars every month and not even realize it. By looking at every single expense, it will allow you to more easily dial back excessive discretionary spending.

Tracking expenses nowadays is easier than ever before thanks to smartphone apps. Find an app by browsing the app marketplace on your smartphone to find something that works for you.

Option 2: Relaxed

If you're like me, you hate wasting money. When I go grocery shopping every week, I will literally stare at two different brands of a food item I'm considering buying and begin calculating the difference in pennies I will save by buying the cheaper food item over the more expensive one. I don't penny pinch because I have too. I do it to save money. If I can save an extra $10 per week on my weekly grocery bill, I save $520 per year. That's the cost of my iPad. I could literally take the savings from penny pinching at the grocery store and buy myself a new iPad every year if I wanted to. Since I'm so diligent about not wasting money, a more "Relaxed" plan works for me.

The relaxed plan relies on you having a pre-set amount of money allocated for each category of your expenses (Rent/mortgage, utilities, car note(s), insurance, groceries, entertainment, discretionary spending, savings, etc.). Once your major expenses have been paid, the rest of your money can be split between savings and discretionary spending.

The real key to this plan that works for me is that I know that each one of my bills is going to generally cost a certain amount of money each month on average. The amount of each bill very seldom fluctuates. I also have a set amount of money I add to my savings account each month. Whatever is left over is mine to spend on discretionary expenditures for that month, or I can choose to roll it over to the next month. The easiest way to think about the Relaxed Plan is to envision three buckets. One bucket is for bills, one bucket is for savings and one bucket is for discretionary spending. Your bills bucket should be about the same each month, which means you should also be able to contribute roughly the same amount to your savings account (bucket) each month. Whatever is left over is placed in your discretionary bucket. If you want, you can go out and frivolously spend your discretionary bucket every month. However, I advise against that because emergencies will always pop up. You may have a medical emergency with a hefty doctor bill or you may have to get work done on your vehicle. It's better to have discretionary money rolled over with a larger amount of money inside to cover these emergency expenses as they pop up. You could pay for these expenses out of your savings account. However, if you get in the habit of doing that, you will never see your savings account increase. Financial emergencies happen and believe me, they happen unexpectedly and more often than you would expect. So be prepared for emergencies, and instead of spending $100 on another pair of jeans or shoes that you really don't need, how about rolling over that $100 back into your discretionary bucket?

How to Split Bills

"It's been estimated that money issues are the driving force in 90% of divorces." (Source: About.com)

Splitting bills and discussing household finances is something that most couples don't discuss. Many men exaggerate how much money they make, leaving them to pay a lion share of the bills without room for much flexibility. Many women don't bother to verify how much money their boyfriend or husband makes, leaving them vulnerable to a financial disaster they never saw coming.

Splitting bills is vital to maintaining a relationship and especially a marriage. Depending on how young you are, you may not perceive this conversation to be of value to you yet, but it should be. You never know when you might fall in love and take the plunge to move in with your significant other. The idea of moving in may sound like one big happy sleep over, until the bills start flowing in.

I've never lived with another woman besides my wife, and thankfully she's just as financially responsible as I am, so I'm fortunate to have a partner I don't have to worry about having financial issues with. We are the exception to the rule. Most couples have tremendous differences in how they view finances and how they split their bills.

Here is the incredibly easy way I recommend splitting bills between couples:

Split your bills based on the percentage of money you each bring into the household. If one of you makes 60% of the household income and the other makes 40% of the household income, split your bills accordingly so that you each pay 60/40 respectively. Here's an example:

Total Monthly Bills: $6,000

- Person A: Earns 60% of household income
- Person A: Pays $3,600 of monthly bills

- Person B: Earns 40% of household income
- Person B: Pays $2,400 of monthly bills

Splitting bills this way ensures that everything remains fair. It doesn't put unnecessary burden on the man just because society says he's supposed to pay all of the bills, and it doesn't require the woman to feel insignificant because she may make less or vice versa.

Many couples who split bills split them 50/50 even though their income differences may be 60/40 or 70/30. If you only make 30% of the household income and are burdened with paying 50% of the bills, this simply isn't fair as it forces you to save tremendously less percentage wise as well as having substantially less discretionary income than your partner who earns 70% of the household income. Don't damage your relationship over money. Split your finances based on proportions and you'll sail through your relationship fair and balanced.

Managing and Monitoring Your Credit

Your credit is the most important thing you have on this planet. Protect it with your life! You know that saying, "your word is your bond?" That pretty much sums up the importance of credit. Your credit scores represent your likelihood to pay back your debts. The most well-known and widely used credit scoring system is the FICO Score. There are three different credit scores for the FICO scoring model that correspond with each of the three national credit bureaus: Equifax, Experian and TransUnion. Each credit bureau's scores are different because they each maintain separate databases with different scoring criteria.

Once a year you can get a free copy of your credit reports as mandated by federal law based on the FACT Act (Fair and Accurate Credit Transactions Act). You can obtain a free copy of your credit reports from all three national bureaus at: annualcreditreport.com. These reports do not contain your credit scores. However, they contain information about your credit history including all open and closed lines of credit. In order to receive your credit scores you will need to use a third-party service.

It's important to pull your credit reports at least once a year to ensure there aren't any inaccurate lines of credit or improper information being reported on your credit reports. Regularly monitoring your credit reports also allows you to ensure your credit hasn't been compromised by identity thieves. Since young adults generally have a limited credit history, they are prime targets for identity thieves because young adults generally have higher credit scores or clean credit as a result of their young age. Identity theft is a real threat and can happen to anyone, including you. Safeguard your credit and consider using a third-party credit monitoring service to provide you with alerts whenever there is an attempt made to open new lines of credit in your name. If you're alerted and take action to notify new creditors and the credit bureaus of fraudulent accounts opened in your name it will make the process of reporting the fraudulent activity and removing the line(s) of credit from your credit reports much easier. Most people fail to regularly monitor their credit reports. Then they go to apply for a new line of credit and they're denied. They thought they had good credit, but unbeknownst to them they had become a victim of identity theft. I know several people of all ages who have been victims of identity theft.

Every single one of them made the mistake of not regularly monitoring their credit reports, until one day they were denied credit and found out that there were delinquent credit lines on their credit reports that were a result of identity theft. Identity theft is a difficult and sometimes impossible problem to solve and creditors rarely side with the victim, especially when a derogatory account has appeared on the persons account for several years. Since the burden of proof lies on the victim, there isn't an easy way to prove that they did not open the negative line(s) of credit. As you can see, identity theft is very serious so be very careful and keep a watchful eye on your credit reports.

Your credit scores dictate the interest rates you will receive on all lines of credit including credit cards, auto loans and home loans. If you're credit score is below a certain level, you could not only receive high interest rates on new lines of credit, but you could also be denied new lines of credit.

I can't explain enough how important it is to build and maintain positive credit scores. In addition to relying upon positive credit scores for big ticket items, many employers now screen candidates based on their credit scores. This means that if you have bad credit (low credit scores), you could lose a job opportunity. In fact, many employers that do credit screenings for new hires also do random credit checks throughout the duration of your employment. Let your credit go bad and you may be terminated from your job. In case you're wondering… Yes. This is totally legal.

Understanding how to use credit can be difficult. Since we're not taught how to use credit in school, it's likely that you'll never learn which is why so many people have bad credit and start their adult lives off with thousands of dollars of debt.

Here are three simple things I've done and continue to do to build and maintain positive credit scores. This may not be 100% correct, but it's what I do and it seems to be working for me:

- Maintain a maximum of three credit card lines:
    - Pay off balances in full every month
    - Use a maximum of 30% of the credit limit on each card every month (credit utilization rate)
- Pay off all outstanding debts including:
    - Student loans
    - Credit cards
    - Medical bills
- Pay all bills on time in full every month

What Next?

I've given you every secret tip and strategy I use for basic financial management. This should get you well on your way to a good start. If you put the basic financial principles to work I've outlined in this chapter, you will live life responsibly, spend money more cautiously, and graduate through life prosperously.

Chapter 9: Message to Parents

Dear Parents,

Listen Up!

Nice Try

Parents. They have the greatest impact and ability to influence the outcome of their children's lives. Sadly, I feel this responsibility is taken too lightly by many parents. I am not yet a parent and I hate to sound like I'm judging parents or pretending I'm an expert on parenting. I'm no expert. However, when looking at my progression into adulthood and looking at my peers I grew up with, there are stark contrasts between how we've turned out that can directly be attributed to parenting. I'm not one to blame or credit parents with the full outcome of their children's lives. However, from what I've witnessed, many parents don't invest enough (if any) time in preparing their children for the real world. It isn't enough to simply tell your kids to "go to school, get good grades, go to college, and get a good job." How does this basic outlook on life provide children with a respect for authority? How does it build character and leadership? How does it teach kids the value of a dollar and how does this basic instruction teach kids how to finance their future?

In this chapter I want to touch on some key points that parents need to hear. If you're a young Millennial and not yet a parent, one day you will likely become a parent so it's important for you to listen up as well because the points I'm about to cover are universal from one generation to the next.

Respect for Authority

Respect for authority. Sadly it's few, far, and in-between when it comes to Millennials, and the generations coming after Millennials are even worse. Just about every time I grocery shop I see a five-year old disobeying their mother because they can't get the cereal of their choice. Instead of disciplining the child, the mother stands there calm and simply takes the abuse. This is unfathomable for me to understand, but I see it happen every weekend. Allowing this behavior to begin at age five and continue on into adulthood is a recipe for building a disrespectful human. If your children don't respect you as parents, how on Earth will they develop respect for other authority figures such as teachers, college professors, or managers?

When I was in middle school we had parent teacher conferences twice a year. Parents came to meet teachers and discuss any issues their kids were having in class. These conferences were open door oriented allowing for parents to come in all at once and go classroom to classroom to meet and discuss issues in a group format. Every time there was a conference there would always be a set of parents that would storm into classrooms and blame the teachers for their kids making failing grades. These parents never once stopped to think that maybe their child didn't study hard enough or pay attention enough in class. They immediately and 100% blamed the teacher. These kids who were in middle school 15 years ago are now total losers. Should you expect anything different? Of course not! When you're 27 years old mommy and daddy can't storm into your boss's office and yell at him or her because he or she is working you too hard or isn't treating you fairly. To make the outcome of these people's lives even worse, as these middle school kids moved on to high school, they no longer needed their parents to storm the building to attack the teacher. The high school student took note from mom and dad after witnessing their tactics and decided they were fit enough to yell at their teachers themselves.

Yep. This is what society has come too. Sure, this isn't a representation of the majority of parents and children. However, as I go to grocery stores and shopping malls on the weekends, I see defiant and disrespectful behavior more and more. If you think our generation was bad, just wait until you see the next one!

Parents. I beg of you. For the sake of your children's future, you must instill in them a respect for authority. Without this vital attribute, your children will be lost in the world disillusioned into believing the world revolves around them.

NEWSFLASH: It doesn't!!!

Building Leaders

Remember when kids used to cut the grass, take out the trash, and do the dishes? It's hard for me to remember because I never witnessed it. I was the only kid in my neighborhood that cut the grass. Everyone else's dad cut the grass. I must admit that I hated cutting the grass, especially during the hot Texas Summer with highs of 110 degrees! As much as I hated it, I later came to realize the reason my dad made me do it. It was to make me appreciate having a lawn to cut as opposed to living in an apartment. The other lesson it taught me was responsibility. When you're 12 years old and you're forced to wake up early on weekends and do something you don't want to do, you gain a sense of life in the real world really quickly. You begin to understand and be better prepared for having to do things you don't want to do as an adult. Who likes getting up early and going to work? Not me, but upon entry into my first real job it was an easy transition for me because I was used to doing things I didn't want to do since I was 12 years old.

Parents. Stop paying a landscaping company to cut the grass. If you have a 12 year old boy in your house, make him cut the grass. That's the least he can do to show his gratitude for the life of luxury you've provided him, and if you have a daughter make her clean the kitchen. I'm not by any means sexist so if you want to reverse the typical gender roles that's fine as well. The point here is to make your kids learn lessons of responsibility at an early age. This is how you build leaders.

Here's another change you should institute. Cut off the unearned allowance. Giving children an allowance for doing nothing creates a false sense of entitlement. If you program a child to believe they deserve free money for doing zero work, they will mooch off of you for the rest of their life. Providing your kids with an allowance to cut the grass and do other household chores is one thing, but giving them an allowance for doing nothing is downright absurd.

Build your kids to be leaders. Teach them responsibility and watch them grow into adulthood with these values they learned ten years prior. They may hate cutting the grass and cleaning the kitchen at 12, but they'll thank you for it at 25.

Valuing the Dollar

What's the power of a dollar? I know it doesn't buy you much these days, which is all the more reason why discussing the value of a dollar is so important. When I was 12 years old my grandfather told me I'd have to work twice as hard to live half as good as he is in his elder years. At the time, I had no idea what he was talking about. As I got older and began working my way into adulthood and paying bills, I quickly realized what my grandfather was talking about.

This section is a continuation of the last section. In the last chapter I mentioned how terrible it is that students go from Kindergarten all the way through college without ever being taught basic financial literacy. Valuing the dollar is the most basic principle of financial literacy and this lesson must be learned in your childhood. In the last chapter I was hyper-critical of the lack of financial literacy in our education system. Despite the lack of in depth financial lessons I would've liked to have learned in school, there was one moment in my school career that did stand out as a means of teaching financial literacy. In the fourth grade, we had a field trip to a place called Enterprise City. The building was setup like a small town with small businesses. Each of the students was assigned a job, given a paycheck, and a check book to balance. In that one day, we walked out of Enterprise City not prepared to take on the world at 11 years old. However, the experience was incredibly valuable and insightful. Enterprise City was unfortunately a program only provided in our local city. As an adult I can't help but to wonder why this isn't a program mandated in schools nationwide. Even though Enterprise City may not be available for your child, you as their parent can easily duplicate the lessons learned. Take time to sit down with your children and show them how to balance a bank account, how to manage finances, and how to allocate money to pay bills. The next time you and your significant other sit down to pay the monthly bills; why not make it a family event. You can even get creative and find ways to "gamify" the financial lesson by providing your kids with fake money or allowance money and rewarding them for balancing their own personal finances. Yes. Your kids have personal finances. They like toys right? They like video games right? Those things cost money and someone has to pay for them. Treat your kids like an adult and give them a job (chores) and pay them for that job. Require them to set aside money for discretionary spending and savings. This will simulate balancing a checking and savings account.

However you teach your children the value of a dollar is up to you. Just be sure you teach them. It doesn't matter if it's playing Monopoly together as a family, sitting your children down beside you while you pay the bills, etc. Just find a way that works that they are receptive too.

I'm not yet a parent and I can imagine that parenting is much more difficult than I can grasp looking in from the outside. However, no matter how difficult parenting may be, it is your responsibility to provide your children with the greatest chance of surviving and thriving in the real world. By enforcing a few basic values and instilling a few key principles, your children will have the skills and attributes they need to prosper.

Conclusion:

The World is ours for the Taking

It's our Time

I don't know about you but everyday I wake up I'm so excited to be alive right now and be apart of this generation-The Millennials. Never before in any generation prior could my story exist. I'm 27 years old and I lack a college education. Based on statistics, I should be earning $20,000 a year working in retail or food services without a glimmer of hope for prosperity, yet somehow I've managed to beat the odds and earn more than triple my "statistical" salary expectations. I'm 27 and have been more than a decade ahead of my time since I was 18 years old. In Corporate America I was always the youngest person in the room by 15 - 20 years. After my first corporate gig I paid off all of my debt based on the plans I outlined in this book. I bought a hot convertible sports car, married my high school sweetheart, moved into a beautiful condo, and I'm now moving onto the next chapter in my life. If you take the steps outlined in this book and put them to action, your story can resemble my story or even better!

This book and my story isn't a celebration for the lack of education. Nor is it a platform for me to brag about my success. The purpose of this book and my story is to inspire an entire generation to see and experience the Real World through my perspective as someone who has experienced and earned things that most people don't obtain until they're well into their 40s.

Life has so many paths to take and no other generation has as many paths of opportunity as Millennials. We have the world at our finger tips and nothing can stop us but ourselves. Never before in any generation prior could someone take their passion and turn it into a business with minimal over head. Never before could someone learn skills for a high paying job in the modern workforce in the comfort of their own home. Never before could an uneducated kid survive and thrive in Corporate America; and never before could a 27 year old tell his story of how he did all of the preceding in a self-published book with global distribution. This is the opportunity we possess. This is the unique time we're living in.

After reading this book, I hope you've gained inspiration and determination to be the best you can be and I hope I've been able to help better prepare you for the Real World. Inspiration is great, but it only takes you so far. After inspiration comes perspiration. I've given you the keys to the kingdom. I've given you every secret I know. Now get ready to sweat, work hard, and grab life by the horns. You are now prepared to survive and thrive in the Real World.

We are The Millennials. It is our time and the world is ours for the taking!

Thank You

I can't begin to thank you enough for reading and spending your hard earned money purchasing this book. There are millions of books to read and somehow you were motivated to buy and read this one. You have no idea how much that means to me.

Selling hundreds, thousands, or even millions of books would be great, but nothing is better than conversing and connecting with those whom I've been able to inspire or assist after reading this book.

If you're a Millennial, a parent of a Millennial, or someone outside of the demographic of this book and you would like to reach out to me please don't hesitate to do so.

I can't wait to hear from you!

"Be The One... To leave behind a legacy; challenge the status quo, and help change a generation forever!"

- Michael Price

- Email: michael@whatnextquest.com
- Website: www.michaelprice.me
- Facebook: www.facebook.com/pricelessmichael
- Twitter: @michaelpriceles (#BeTheOne)

Appendix A: Checklist

Remembering all of the individual bits and pieces of a book can be rather challenging. Since this book was written as a guide, I thought I'd provide you with a checklist of key points from each chapter of the book to make things a little easier. This checklist is not a replacement for reading the book, but rather a supplement.

1. Leverage the Internet

- Education: Take eCourses to advance and sharpen your skills through online education services such as: Lynda.com, Mixergy.com, Udemy.com and Khanacademy.com.

- Social Networking: Develop professional social networks, follow influencers within your field and keep in touch.

- Real World Networking: Meet real people in person. Attend networking events and connect with like-minded people.

- Build a Business: Consider building an online business based on a hobby or a passion.

2. High School

- Aptitude: Take a general aptitude test to determine how your natural abilities align with specific career paths. Rinse and repeat this process every year of high school and beyond. Ideally, this process begins in Elementary school.

- Extracurricular: Get involved in extracurricular activities that align with your aptitude and expand your intellect.

- Volunteer: Take time out to make a difference in other peoples' lives. Volunteer at an organization you have an emotional/personal connection with.

- Intern: Become an intern for one or more companies in an industry you'd like to explore as a career option.

3. Higher Education

- Explore: Look within yourself and determine the value of higher education based on your career choice and career objectives.

4. Build a Brand

- Blog: Start a blog and develop regularly posted content based on your career interests.

- Social Networking: Continue further development of your social networks as mentioned in step 1.

- Portfolio: Develop a professional website portfolio including: internships, volunteering details, references, education, skills, achievements and a copy of your resume'.

- Work: Work for free (if necessary) to add as much experience to your resume' and portfolio as possible.

5. Joining the Workforce

- Roles: Know who you are within your company and maintain a level-head.

- Worth: Continually assess your value to ensure you're appropriately being compensated and valued based on your position within your industry.

- Climb: Get in good with your colleagues and upper

management to illustrate your value and secure your position.

- Value: Be valuable at all times to develop greater job security.

- Leadership: Be a leader. Lead yourself and when asked, lead others.

- Synergy: Help create company culture by working to bring people together for greater efficiency and cohesiveness.

6. Exit the Workforce
(Optional: Pursue at your own risk!)

- Preparation: Learn business.

- Save: Establish a savings fund prior to your exit from the workforce to fund your business and personal expenses.

- Plan: Establish a plan to build your business and evaluate your risk.

- Build: Build your business.

7. Financial Literacy

Note: Financial literacy should really begin in high school or even as early as elementary school. However, given the flow of the book, this part of the process will be placed here to keep with the flow of the content within this book.

- Plan: Develop a spending/savings plan that suits your objectives for your short-term and long-term expenses.

- Track: Track and monitor your expenses based on a plan that works for you.

- Monitor: Monitor and manage your credit to ensure you maintain a positive credit history.

Appendix B: Resources

Books

Your brain is like a sponge. Soak it up with as much knowledge as you can. Provided here is a list of books I've read that have helped influence my approach to business, life, and personal finance. I hope they help you as much as they've helped me.

Business:

Title: Think and Grow Rich
Author: Napoleon Hill

Title: The Art of the Deal
Author: Donald Trump

Title: Purple Cow
Author: Seth Godin

Title: All Marketers are Liars
Author: Seth Godin

Title: Tribes We Need You to Lead Us
Author: Seth Godin

Title: FREE: The Future of a Radical Price
Author: Chris Anderson

Title: The Cluetrain Manifesto
Author: David Weinberger, David Searls, Christopher Locke, Rick Levine

Title: Crush It!
Author: Gary Vaynerchuk

Title: The Thank You Economy
Author: Gary Vaynerchuk

Title: Rework
Author: Jason Fried, David Heinemeier Hansson

Title: Nine Things Successful People Do Differently
Author: Heidi Grant Halvorson

Title: The 4-Hour Work Week
Author: Timothy Ferriss

Title: Launch
Author: Michael A. Stelzner

Title: Rich Dad, Poor Dad
Author: Robert Kiyosaki

Motivational:

Title: Don't Sweat the Small Stuff, and It's All Small Stuff
Author: Richard Carlson, Ph.D

Title: The Magic of Believing
Author: Claude M. Bristol

Title: The Magic of Thinking Big
Author: David J. Schwartz, Ph.D

Title: The Tipping Point: How Little Things Can Make a Big Difference
Author: Malcolm Gladwell

Personal Finance:

Title: The Money Book for the Young, Fabulous & Broke
Author: Suze Orman

Title: The Millionaire Next Door
Author: Thomas J. Stanley, Ph.D, William D. Danko, Ph.D

Title: The Total Money Makeover
Author: Dave Ramsey

Websites and Services

The Internet is incredible! That's why I dedicated an entire chapter in this book to discussing it. Provided here is a list of websites for various functions that you can use to simplify, improve, and enhance your life.

Business/Career:

Name: Salary.com
URL: www.salary.com

Name: Mixergy
URL: www.mixergy.com

Name: OnStartups
URL: www.onstartups.com

Name: Entrepreneur
URL: www.entrepreneur.com

Name: Inc. Magazine Guides
URL: www.inc.com/guides

Name: Under 30 CEO
URL: www.under30ceo.com

Social Media:

Name: Mashable
URL: www.mashable.com

Name: Problogger.net
URL: www.problogger.net

Name: Social Media Examiner
URL: www.socialmediaexaminer.com

Name: All Facebook
URL: www.allfacebook.com

Name: Social Media Today
URL: www.socialmediatoday.com

eLearning:

Name: Lynda.com
URL: www.lynda.com

Name: Code Academy
URL: www.codeacademy.com

Name: Udemy
URL: www.udemy.com

Name: Khan Academy
URL: www.khanacademy.com

Name: Bright Storm
URL: www.brightstorm.com

Name: Tuts Plus
URL: www.tutsplus.com

Personal Finance:

Name: Mint
URL: www.mint.com

Name: My Fico
URL: www.myfico.com

Name: Wise Bread
URL: www.wisebread.com

Name: Fool
URL: www.fool.com

Appendix C: Research

I give credit where credit is due. Provided below are the research sources I used for this book. Check out these links for even more detailed information about the subjects related to this book.

Millennials are young adults born between: Author unlisted, "Generation Y," Wikipedia.org, March 25, 2013. www.en.wikipedia.org/wiki/Generation_Y

Who knows only his own generation: Author unlisted, "George Norlin (1871-1942)," Colorado.edu, Publish date unlisted. www.ucblibraries.colorado.edu/about/norlin.htm

46% of Millennials between the ages: Charles B. Stockdale and Michael B. Sauter, "Eight Products the Facebook Generation Will Not Buy," Foxbusiness.com, April 19, 2012. www.foxbusiness.com/technology/2012/04/19/eight-products-facebook-generation-will-not-buy/

80% of college students change: Author unlisted, "When Your College Student Changes Majors," Collegeparents.org, Publish date unlisted. www.collegeparents.org/members/resources/articles/when-your-college-student-changes-majors

59% of Americans surveyed have reported: Author unlisted, "How Do Americans Feel about Their Jobs?," Businesswire.com, August 29, 2012. www.businesswire.com/news/home/20120829005887/en

2% of college athletes go pro: Tony Manfred, "Here Are The Odds That Your Kid Becomes A Professional Athlete (Hint: They're Small)," Businessinsider.com, February 10, 2012. www.businessinsider.com/odds-college-athletes-become-professionals-2012-2?op=1

35% of students who enter college: ccrzadkiewicz, "Why do Students Drop Out of College?," Brighthub.com, February 8, 2012. www.brighthub.com/education/college/articles/82378.aspx

63% of students who enroll: Jeanne Sahadi, "College in 4 years? Try 5 or 6.," Cnn.com, June 22, 2004. www.money.cnn.com/2004/06/21/pf/college/graduation_rates/

37% of students will either drop out: ccrzadkiewicz, "Why do Students Drop Out of College?," Brighthub.com, February 8, 2012. www.brighthub.com/education/college/articles/82378.aspx

Kim Kardashian has been reported: Tammy Todd, "Twitter stunned Kim Kardashian earns $10k a tweet," Examiner.com, December 29, 2009. www.examiner.com/article/twitter-stunned-kim-kardashian-earns-10k-a-tweet

You may like drawing stick figures: Author unlisted, "I Want To Draw A Cat For You Season 3 Episode," Sharktanksuccess.blogspot.com, Publish date unlisted. www.sharktanksuccess.blogspot.com

Nearly half of Americans have less: Harry Bradford, "Nearly Half Of Americans Have Less Than $500 In Savings: Survey," Huffingtonpost.com, October 22, 2012. www.huffingtonpost.com/2012/10/22/americans-savings-500_n_2003285.html

Only 14% of American workers: John Reeves, "17 Frightening Facts About Retirement Savings in America," Fool.com, October 15, 2012. www.fool.com/retirement/general/2012/10/15/17-frightening-facts-about-retirement-savings-in-.aspx

Nearly 75% of retirees have not: John Reeves, "17 Frightening Facts About Retirement Savings in America," Fool.com, October 15, 2012. www.fool.com/retirement/general/2012/10/15/17-frightening-facts-about-retirement-savings-in-.aspx

56% of workers report that: John Reeves, "17 Frightening Facts About Retirement Savings in America," Fool.com, October 15, 2012. www.fool.com/retirement/general/2012/10/15/17-frightening-facts-about-retirement-savings-in-.aspx

30% of Americans say: Jason Hull, "The Middle Class Retirement Delusion By the Numbers," Usnews.com, December 21, 2012. www.money.usnews.com/money/blogs/the-smarter-mutual-fund-investor/2012/12/21/the-middle-class-retirement-delusion-by-the-numbers

49% of Americans say: Blake Ellis, "49% of Americans saving zilch for retirement," Cnn.com, May 10, 2012. www.money.cnn.com/2012/05/10/retirement/saving-retire/index.htm

Attend community college: Jeffery King, "5 Reasons Community Colleges Make Sense Right Now," Usnews.com, May 30, 2012. www.money.usnews.com/money/blogs/my-money/2012/05/30/5-reasons-community-colleges-make-sense-right-now

Live at home while: Farnoosh Torabi, "Ways to Attend College For Free," Yahoo.com, August 6, 2012. www.finance.yahoo.com/news/ways-to-attend-college-for-free.html

According to The Bureau: Barbara Safani, "Could You Have Seven New Careers in One Lifetime?," Aol.com, September 10, 2010. www.jobs.aol.com/articles/2010/09/10/new-careers/

It's been estimated that money: Deborah Fowles, "Couples and Money," About.com, Publish date unlisted. www.financialplan.about.com/cs/familyfinances/a/CouplesMoney.htm

Your credit score is: Author unlisted, "Credit score in the United States," Wikipedia.com, Publish date unlisted. www.en.wikipedia.org/wiki/Credit_score_in_the_United_States

CPSIA information can be obtained at www.ICGtesting.com
Printed in the USA
BVOW03s2030090415

395520BV00002B/34/P

9 780989 294713